LOOK

TO THE

HILLS

A Prescription to
Cure the Real Issues of Life

BISHOP DARRYL S. BRISTER

Tulsa, Oklahoma

LOOK TO THE HILLS

Look to the Hills by Bishop Darryl S. Brister

Published by Insight Publishing Group
8801 S. Yale, Suite 410
Tulsa, OK 74137
918-493-1718

Unless otherwise noted, all Scripture quotations are from the New King James version of the Bible. Copyright © 1979, 1980, 1982 by Thomas Nelson, Inc., publishers. Scriptures marked KJV are taken from the King James Version of the Bible.

ISBN 1-930027-71-0
Library of Congress catalog card number: 2002110998

Printed in the United States of America

INTRODUCTION

One of the most challenging aspects of walking in the footsteps of the Risen King is that many times we've got to endure more than we enjoy. Unfortunately, the Church at large has promoted recognition more than relationship. I've written this book to equip those who are serious about a dedicated relationship with Jesus Christ.

In this book you'll notice I addressed some of the common maladies that bring challenges to the personal lives of believers. In Psalm 121:1-2 the psalmist records, *"I will lift up my eyes to the hills-from whence comes my help? My help comes from the lord, who made heaven and earth."* If you read this in proper context you can almost hear the personal struggle in the life of the Psalmist. The hills that the writer sees are the hills of Zion and Jerusalem, the Old Testament symbol for the dwelling place of God.

If you ever put your faith, hope, and trust in anything or anyone else other than God you've set yourself up for a faith failure, because it or them will fail. The revelatory instruction that comes to us in this present season is simply, "Look to the Hills!" As you read, allow the Holy Spirit to nail the revelation on the wall of your heart. Pray each prayer and watch God move on your behalf.

DEDICATION

I'd like to dedicate this work to those who are responsible for shaping and molding me into the man of God that I am today.

First of all, to my father and mentor who is now in heaven, the late Ellie D. Brister, Sr.

To my first pastor, the late Rev. Dr. Freddie H. Dunn, Sr.

To my god-mother, Elizabeth Davis, who slipped away the other day from labor to reward.

Bishop Paul S. Morton, Sr., my father in the gospel.

Bishop Nathaniel Holcomb, my father in the faith.

To all of my sons and daughters in the ministry who allow me to speak into their lives on a daily, weekly, and monthly basis.

To my wife and children who willingly share me with the masses.

To the Family of Light and the staff of DSB Ministries, you are the greatest.

TABLE OF CONTENTS

CHAPTER ONE

WORRY: MISUSED IMAGINATION

Some of you are glad you picked this book up already! God has a word for you! At the very outset, I want to give to you a definition for the word *worry*, because many of us need to understand that worrying is a spirit. It is a spirit of worry. The word *worry* comes from an Old English term "wyrgan." This term means "to choke" or "to strangle." That's exactly what the spirit of worry does in the life a believer! It will strangle you literally to death, and I'm going to show you that.

Another interesting way of thinking about worry is that it is misused imagination. We all have to deal with problems in our lives every day, and God knows that many of us have issues that are worthy of concern. We are going to develop this in order to understand what the enemy does to capitalize on any opportunity he can to make your life miserable.

We have all been or are presently tempted by the desires of this world—we allow the natural things in life that we crave, work for and earn. Understand that God doesn't have anything against us obtaining possessions; the problem that God has is when our possessions have *us* instead of us having them.

All of us are tempted by material possessions. For some of us it's clothes or cars, for others it might be a relationship or a career. All of us battle certain selfish desires to pay attention to the tangible possessions of this world. It's okay to have things, but you must make sure that when you can't have certain things it doesn't alter you as an individual.

Let me ask you a question: Do you worry about how to keep what you've got—your possessions, your health, your status, or your position? Jesus tells us that if at any time you become overwhelmed by the cares of this life, you must change your focus.

There is a tremendous difference between worrying and being concerned, and I'm not suggesting that you should no longer expect to experience issues common to humanity and have things that concern you. What I am saying, however, is that you must avoid being overly concerned so that your attitude, prayer life, and relationship with God and others doesn't change.

Matthew 6:19 is so familiar to some of us, I'm afraid that we may miss the profundity of what Jesus is saying. It says:

> Do not lay up for yourselves treasures on earth, where moth and rust destroy and where thieves break in and steal; but lay up for yourselves treasures in heaven, where neither moth nor rust destroys and where thieves

do not break in and steal. For where your treasure is there your heart will be also.

I find this very interesting because Jesus is saying that everything that comes from the world and everything in the world has "temporary" stamped on it. He is telling us to focus our attention on things that are eternal; He is talking about perspective and perception, as it relates to the things of life. Jesus tells us not to be concerned with earthly goods but instead to be interested in *eternal* treasures.

Some of you have had your health affected, your emotional stability, your personality, even your spiritual walk with God—all interrupted because you're on a quest for things; the things on earth, rather than the things of heaven. You may have picked up this book today worried about a number of things: issues with your job, your marriage, what the doctor had to say, or even your kids' situation. All of these things are legitimate reasons to be concerned; however, when you begin to be consumed with worry, these situations start to strangle you, and they can literally choke you!

These are the principles God is establishing: He says, where your treasure is, there will your heart be also. Now watch this; in verse 25 of the same chapter:

Therefore I say to you, do not worry about your life, what you will eat or what you will drink; nor about your body, what you will put on. Is not life more than food and the body more than clothing? Look at the birds of the air, for they neither sow nor reap nor gather into barns; yet your heavenly Father feeds them. Are you not of more value than they? Which of you by worrying can add one cubic to his stature? So why do you worry about clothing? Consider the lilies of the field, how they grow: they neither toil nor spin; and yet I say to you that even Solomon in all his glory was not arrayed like one of these. Now if God so clothed the grass of the field, which today is, and tomorrow is thrown into the oven, will he not much more clothe you, O you of little faith? Therefore do not worry, saying, "What shall we eat?" or "What shall we drink?" or "What shall we wear?" For after all of these things the gentiles seek. For your heavenly Father knows that you need all these things. But seek first the kingdom of God and His righteousness, and all these things shall be added to you.

Christians: We have to change our perceptions; we have to change our focus. Jesus is explicit that we are not to worry! In verse 30, He describes those who worry about mundane things as being of little faith; which means, if you are caught up or dominated by a spirit of worry, it's obvious you lack faith.

The individual who is dominated by the spirit of worry is a person who needs to pray, "Lord, increase my faith!" When you worry about issues over which you have no control, you're saying not with your mouth but with your very thoughts—is that you lack confidence in God's ability to deal with the situation and to bring you through.

Some of you are allowing worry dominate your minds and you are losing sleep, and your appetite or you may be walking nights away or baptizing your pillow with tears every night—all for something you can't do anything about.

However, here's something to use against the enemy when he tries to dominate your life, health, and emotions as he attempts to crash your spiritual walk: go back in your mind and remember a time your back was up against the wall—and you didn't know how you'd ever get out of it—but God supernaturally made a way for you.

> *The individual who is dominated by the spirit of worry is a person who needs to pray.*

The person who is worrying is the person who has just gotten into a relationship with God. Because when you've walked with God for some time, you learn to say, "Lord, I don't know how I'm going to pay those bills; but when it's time for me to sleep, I'll leave it in your hands, and I'm not taking them to bed with me." Or you might say, "I don't know what's happening at work, but I'm going to let You do the driving, and I'm going to enjoy the view from the backseat." Know that God can take care of your concerns so you can sleep. The Bible tells us that He that keeps Israel neither slumbers nor sleeps. Jesus is going to be up anyway, so you might as well not stay up worrying about it; He'll take care of it while you sleep! Lay hands on yourself and say, "Lord, increase my faith!"

Jesus says don't worry. He says that you should put your concerns in proper perspective. Look at the birds, He says! Your heavenly Father feeds them; and you're of more value than any bird! Birds don't have jobs; they don't have bank accounts, or savings, and a bird doesn't know where his next meal is going to come from. But despite the number of birds you see outside, He makes sure they find worms to make it from day to day, and Jesus is saying that if God makes sure a *bird* gets his needs met, surely you must understand that He'll make sure your needs are met too!

> *God wants us to be free from the worry and anxiety that can rule our daily lives.*

So what are you worried about?

God provides food for birds, and He clothes the flowers of the field. Let's make a parallel here between birds and flowers: God takes care of them so that you'll understand you have nothing to fear, because He cares much more for you than he does plants and animals! He knows what we need, and He'll give it to us both now and for eternity.

God wants us to be free from the worry and anxiety that can rule our daily lives. He's saying, "What are you worrying for? If you can't pay your bills, what's worrying going to do for you?"

When we allow a spirit of worry to rule our lives, we open ourselves to the trick of the enemy: if he can't get in through one area, he'll use another. He says, "Now that your finances are all messed up, I can get in here!" The bills are coming due, and he whispers in your ear, "It's almost the 15th! What are you going to do? You're already two months behind; there goes your credit!" Or, "You're almost 40 and you're not married; all your friends are married, and the good men are gone!

Besides, who'll marry you with kids?" "You heard your boss; they're talking about laying people off! You're next, the job is gone!"

What has happened? The enemy has gotten you to listen to him and to concentrate on yourself. He's got your thoughts so cluttered with worry that you can't have creative ideas, and now you're using up all your energy focusing on problems. The enemy hopes that he can throw your life out of balance; he doesn't care where he gets his foot in the door.

Don't allow the enemy get you so preoccupied that you can't make right decisions on important issues. Sometimes your bills aren't late because you don't have the money; they're late because you spent so much time worrying, your brain got cluttered and you forgot where you put the bill! When your mind is cluttered, you feel indecisive. You're so worried about making the wrong decision, sometimes you don't make any decisions!

Financial insecurity accounts for a lot of worries, even in the Church. It drives some people to become workaholics. For others, you know that you need a certain amount to live and know you will bring home less than that, so before you even take your paycheck home, you're already short for the month.

Don't you think the enemy knows that if you're making three thousand dollars a month and only need two thousand to live, he'll have a harder time tempting you not to tithe? It's one thing to write out a tithe check by faith; it's completely another to *know* that you've got enough to tithe—and to even give extra! If the enemy can throw off your giving, he can mess with one of the greatest ways God uses to bless us.

Instead of being above your situation, with God, you're indecisive and overly concerned; now you're getting a bad attitude—you're frustrated and aggravated. Everything gets on your nerves, and maybe you're even tempted to panic. Perhaps you're beginning to feel depressed; you're now open to a spirit of depression. You're then negative, which comes directly from the spirit of worry. When you are bound by the spirit of worry, you become very critical. You find fault in everyone else. Worry produces a judgmental spirit and causes us to become controlling. It all comes from a spirit of worry!

Understand that your troubles are often God preparing you for something. When you go before the Lord, be mindful that all things work together for good to those who love the Lord and walk according to His purpose. God may not have the victory in mind for you so much as for someone you might share with later. You can tell them later how God brought you out. Thank God for your enemies, because the Word says He'll make a table for you amid all of your enemies!

Many of us are bound in this area because we don't have our eyes on Jesus—we have them on other people. The enemy wants you to look at others and try to get what they have, to prove that you are just as sufficient as they are. But God says we're to get our eyes off of earthly things and onto heavenly things. If we seek His kingdom first, all of the other things will come after *you!* Look to the hills . . .

You may see what I've got now, but you didn't see what I went through to get what God has entrusted me with. Before you ask for what another person has, you must be willing to go through what they've gone through to receive it. Many of us

14

want the fruit, but we don't want to plant the seed and water the tree. You don't get the fruit without first planting the seed.

God may be saying, "Why should I give you more money? You don't tithe from what you receive now! Until you show me that I can trust you with more"—more of anything— "you'll have to trust Me with what you have."

As a result of our unwillingness to put in the effort, we're often full of worry, jealousy, backbiting, and envy; and then you're mad at someone else because they have what you want, but you're unwilling to do what they did in order to get it.

Virtually nothing happens overnight. If you see someone driving a new car—perhaps the one you want to drive—maybe you should find out what they're doing to get their life in order. You might find out they are

> *God may have blessings in store for you that you can't have at this point in your life.*
> *Not now doesn't mean not at all!*

making the same money you are and are driving that new car. You might just need to get order to what you have so that you can see the difference between a want, a need, and a desire. God may have blessings in store for you that you can't have at this point in your life.

It is easy to find fault in other people and to be envious of their blessings. If you're not careful, the spirit of worry can cause you to isolate yourself until you're lonely, self-centered, and worrying all the time while those around you are blessed by God!

Worrying is misused imagination. God has given us an imagination. Do you sometimes see what God is bringing you

15

toward? You don't know how, but you know you'll get there, and you can see it! You may not have a dollar or even a dime to make it happen, but you see it in your spirit. God gives us visions, and worrying is misuse of that! You have to be able to turn the

God gives us visions, and worrying is misuse of that!

tables on the enemy. Don't let him use the ability to see the visions God gave you to make you see disaster. Instead, tell yourself, "I don't know how it will get done, but if God says it, that's enough for me! I don't know how God will do it, but He *will* do it."

God wants us to arrive at the point where we realize we don't have all the answers, but He does. Understand that His promises are clear, but sometimes His procedure is cloudy. I often times don't know how it will happen, but if God said it, then He will do it, and I'm going to live as though His promise has already come true!

Think big! Go for what God is promising you! You're His; you deserve the best, and don't settle for anything less. God knows that when He blesses you, you'll open your big mouth and will tell everyone how good He is! You'll tell people it wasn't because you were lucky, or because you're so good looking, or because you've got financial savvy; you'll tell them it's because God gave you favor!

He's telling you to delight yourself in Him, and He'll give you the desires of your heart. Get your eyes off the cars, the women, men, and the job! Get your eyes on God. Seek His kingdom. Tell yourself that you're through worrying. Turn it over to Jesus! Give Him your worries, and He will give you His peace. Your bills may be due, but you'll have His peace; you may still not have a dime, but He'll give you peace.

You can't add an inch to your height by worrying, so why do we do it? If God clothes the grass of the field, which is here today and gone tomorrow, will He not care for you? People who don't have their hope and confidence in Jesus worry about what they're going to eat and drink and wear. Father God already knows what you need, and He's promised to supply all your needs! Just think: if you got that job, that car, that husband or wife, and yet still didn't have God, you'd have nothing but problems!

Dr. Charles Mills, the co-founder of the Mayo Clinic, pointed out how worry affects the entire body. He said it affects the circulatory system; it affects your heart, your glands, and your nervous system. Dr. Mills used to say that he never knew of anyone who died from overwork, but he knew of many who had died from worry. Worry will only shorten your days. You can't worry yourself into a longer or happier life.

Do you know that if the enemy had his way, you would be dead? The enemy wants to take you out before you discover and walk in your purpose and blessing. He knows he may not be able to get you to commit adultery, but if he can convince you to worry, he can take you out early and rob you of what God has for you.

Philippians 4:4 says:

Rejoice in the Lord always. Again I will say, rejoice! Let your gentleness be known to all men. The Lord is at hand. Be anxious for nothing, but in everything by prayer and supplication, with thanksgiving, let your requests be made known to God; and the peace of God, which surpasses all understanding, will guard your hearts and minds through Christ Jesus.

The Scripture above explains why many of us can't seem to get our requests through to God; we're not praying the way God intends. It says that we're not supposed to be anxious but to ask with thanksgiving. We often go to God saying, "Oh, Jesus! These bills! These children!" and we think that because we're crying, we'll get God's attention. God says that we're supposed to come to Him in thanksgiving, saying, "My heart is hurt, but I'm thanking You for what I'm going through."

Often we don't make our requests known; we just whine about our problems. We say, "Lord, give me a break-through!" and He says, "Breakthrough for what? Tell Me what you are going through." We say, "Lord, I'm believing it's mine," and He's saying, "What's yours?" We aren't specific in our requests, and we despise being specific in our repentance. We say, "Lord, forgive me!" God says, "Forgive you for what? You committed your sins one by one, so name them one by one." God will give you wisdom for what to ask, so get the wisdom, and then be specific! Make your requests known to God. Understand that just a little talk with Jesus will make everything all right.

I want to give you four steps to diagnose and analyze your worries.

First, take it one day at a time. We often smother our today with worries about tomorrow and regrets for yesterday. We kill today! That's why Jesus tells us not to worry about tomorrow; tomorrow will take care of itself. Don't allow your present worries to eclipse what God has for you tomorrow. Tomorrow belongs to God!

Second, get the facts. Take the time to figure out specifically what you're worried about. Write down your worries, and then consider how much good contemplating the problem will do you. When you become a real follower of God, you'll begin to trust Him and you'll see Him at work; this will cause your perspective and perception to change.

Third, analyze the results. As you look at what your concern accomplishes, you'll see that it isn't the situation that's got you distressed; it's the worry and the anticipation. Change this with thanksgiving to help you put Him first and trust in His goodness and kindness toward you. You can either worry yourself to death, or you can give it over to God and have His peace.

Fourth, improve upon the worst. Now that you have it set out in front of you, you know what is really worrying you. Take positive steps to prevent the most negative results—give thanks, praise God, and think first of His kingdom.

As an example of this fourth step, one of the members of my church was running for public office. However, one day he called and told me that he was withdrawing from the race. He said that he had discovered he couldn't afford to lose. He had taken a certain amount out of his savings, and he knew that if he didn't win, he wouldn't be able to try again and it would have a negative effect on his family. As his pastor, I could have said, "You should just have faith," etcetera. But what he was saying was he wasn't ready; if he was ready, he would have had more money, and then he could have afforded to lose. By planning against the worst, however, he prepared for next time—when he would be ready.

When God gives you vision, He gives you provision. Many of us confuse common sense with a lack of faith. Be careful not to get ahead of God, because many times when we fail it's because we have taken a high seat at the table, but it's not our season. God will show you what is yours, where He's taking you—and if He isn't leading, it's not unusual that you're worried because you're off on your own!

Don't get impatient and get ahead of God, because it will cost you severely. That's what happened to Abraham and Sarah. God said He would bless them with a child. Abraham had plenty of faith; Romans 4:21 says that he was fully convinced that what God "had promised He was also able to perform."

Many of us are aware of what God has promised, but we aren't convinced of His ability to perform! We know He said it, but we're shaky on believing He'll do it. We often feel as though we need to help God out. Abraham had confidence in God's ability, but Sarah wasn't so sure. She convinced Abraham that God needed some help, and Ishmael was the result—and Ishmael means "product of the flesh." Ishmael is what you produce when you don't wait on God.

Have you ever produced any Ishmaels? Look at how much strife there is between the Jews and the Arabs; sons of the flesh against sons of promise. Ishmaels will always cause you heartache and pain, and they're a result of being unable to wait on God. Not now doesn't mean not at all.

Don't let worry choke you; don't allow the desires of your flesh to cause you to be greedy and envy others that God is blessing. Instead, have faith that He is able to perform that which He has promised. Ask God to increase your faith, remembering that He provides food for little birds and clothing for the flowers in the fields. You're of much more value than a sparrow or a flower! The enemy will use your worries to gain inroads into your life, to make you sick, anxious, and confused. He'll make you desire what others have instead of being willing to wait on God's blessings. He'll make you want to step out and "help God," but instead of helping, you will produce a son of your flesh—an Ishmael. However, as you make your requests known to God, as you talk to Him, He will give you the desires of your heart, and He will provide!

So don't worry!

Now before we go any further pray this prayer with me:

"Father in the name of Jesus, I'm convinced that you are in complete control of my life. You know what I'm going through right now, I ask that you would please increase my faith. Help me to understand that nothing that has happened in my life has caught you by surprise. Worrying is not of you, so I denounce the spirit of worrying and I embrace the trust in you that has brought me to where I am. Thank you for deliverance in the name of Jesus! Amen."

CHAPTER TWO

ANGER: A NATURAL EMOTION

M any of us already know before I begin to share on the subject of anger, it is a word in season. We are in a unique season right now, and I'm encouraged to see what the end is going to be.

1 John 4:4 in the King James Version says, "Ye are of God, little children, and have overcome them, because He who is in you is greater than he that is in the world."

First of all, I want you to understand that anger is a natural emotion. God created us with our senses, and understand this at the outset—when God creates us and saves us, he doesn't dehumanize us or take away our individuality when we experience sanctification. I want you to understand that although you are saved, you still have to live a very real life.

There will be some things that will cause your nature to respond, and one of them is a spirit of anger. Can you think of anything that made you angry since you have been saved? You should be able to; I sure can! So we understand that anger is a natural emotion.

This is what the Word says in the book of Ephesians: "Be ye angry and sin not." In other words, the Lord says there is nothing wrong with being angry, but you should not allow your anger to provoke you to sin. That is the ultimate objective of the enemy. The enemy seeks for opportunities where he can hinder and affect your witness.

Psalms 7:11 says, "God is a just judge, and God is angry with the wicked everyday." I want you to know that anger is a natural emotion. You can sit in church and act like a super saint, but there are still things in your life that will really make you angry.

You have to understand that anger is a spirit. Let me bring some things alive for you: I want to show you how normal anger is. The almighty God himself has gotten angry. In Numbers 11:1, the Bible says, "Now when the people complained, it displeased the Lord; for the Lord heard it, and His anger was aroused." I believe in the King James Version it says, "when his anger was kindled," but in the NKJV it says, "when the people complained, it displeased the Lord; The Lord heard their complaining, and His anger was aroused. So the fire of the Lord burned among them, and consumed some in the outskirts of the camp." Verse ten says, "Then Moses heard the people weeping throughout their families, everyone at the door of his tent; and the anger of the Lord was greatly aroused; Moses also was displeased."

I want you to see that even God himself got angry. There is nothing wrong with getting angry, but the important thing is that we do not allow our anger to provoke us to sin.

When you get saved, the way you handle a situation or problem should be a bit different than the way an unbeliever handles the same issue. Even when things come into your life to make you upset, your response should be different now that Jesus Christ is living on the inside. Remember, greater is He that is in you than he that is in the world!

There are evil spirits that lurk about us. Understand that the enemy will use whatever he possibly can to get you out of the will of God. Some of you who are reading this really need to be delivered from the spirit of anger—uncontrollable anger.

What I want you to see is how you can please God in every season and every setting within your life, and to help accomplish that, I want to give you a definition of anger: "Anger is a sudden feeling of displeasure and antagonism in response to an irritating factor."

The irritation may have been felt for some time, but anger is almost always an eruptive response—whether you are saved or not. It's like an active volcano; from a distance it looks like a wonderful hill, but deep inside the core there is something going on. And then one day, there is an eruption, and hot lava is going everywhere! That's the way the spirit of anger is.

Anger isn't a planned response; you don't leave home and say to yourself, "Today I am going to get mad." Sometimes anger just erupts, and before you realize you're losing it, you've lost it.

A person or a situation may create the irritating factor. But many times, a given situation or person isn't even responsible for the eruption. Often an eruption of anger is caused by an irritation that was lying dormant on the inside.

Here's the trouble with anger: The angry person is momentarily out of control, and he is no longer operating according to God's principles of love. Have you been angry this month? Have you been angry this week? Were you angry today? You might even be mad right now. Let me give you three reasons people tend to get angry:

The first is because they aren't allowed to have their way. Here's an example: A husband and wife that walk around pouting. They both got *older* but neither of them ever grew up! Most marriages fail because of selfishness. It's not a lack of love; they simply are not allowed to have their way, respectively. Many of us were just like this when we were children; if things didn't go our way, we pouted. Many of us are acting like immature Christians: we're singing and shouting dancing and prophesying to the people of God, but God is saying to us that we've got to grow up before we go up!

The second reason people get angry is that they are in pain—either physical or emotional pain. When an individual is in pain—physical or emotional—they often give place to the spirit of anger. The pain can even be from all the way back in their childhood! People become angry quickly because they can't have their way, and because they're in pain.

Finally, people get angry because they are jealous. An angry person many times is a jealous person. I call them Twenty-First Century "player-haters." They are full of anger because they see someone else that has something they wish they had. They won't say they are jealous or envious of how God has moved in your life, but they are. Whenever God begins to bless you and you walk in the blessings of God, your "player-haters" will increase.

Right now there are people upset with you that don't even *know* you. It's because of who you are, where you are, and where you are going. They see that you have something on the inside of you that they don't have on the inside of them, and they are not man or woman enough to ask you, "How do I get what you have?" So instead they are jealous. Some of you jealous people are reading this. Stop trying to fit in, because you don't fit!

There are people in the church that don't like you because they can't get their hair like yours; they don't like you because of your size; they don't like you because of your personality; they don't like you because of your demeanor, or because of what you drive or who you are engaged to or where you are headed; they don't like you because of where you live, and it fills them with jealousy. They don't like you, and they don't even know you!

Angry people are often selfish, in pain, and jealous.

Don't worry about these people, they are losing sleep over you, and you don't even know they exist. I'm writing from experience. Half the people that lie about me and talk about me don't know me. Angry people are often selfish, in pain, and jealous.

Anger is an area in which I have experienced deliverance. I had such a temper! How many of you are like me and sometimes you want to say, "Lord, please let me lay aside my spirituality and let me give them a piece of my mind!" Thank God for growth!

Some people are just walking around like a time bomb. They are just angry. They don't get along with *anybody*. They want to size everybody up. There are some people that you can just look at and tell they are mean! However, when you understand the Holy Ghost is living on the inside of you, you can love the "hell" right out of anybody—and you can manage your anger, no matter what they are like.

You can put this book down and walk away in rebellion, but the Lord will deal with you justly. And if you accept what I'm saying, you can be sure that as soon as you finish reading, this word is going to be tested—on the job, at home, while you're driving. The devil will push a button to make you go off.

Proverbs 14:17 says, "A quick-tempered man acts foolishly, and a man of wicked intentions is hated." Are you a quick-tempered man (or woman)? Does everything make you mad? Is something always wrong? Does the smallest thing make you lose it? The Holy Ghost says you need to check yourself before you wreck yourself. Quick-tempered men act foolishly. The King James Version says it this way: "The man that is soon angry dealeth foolishly, and a man of wicked devices is hated." People that live foolishly are called fools.

The Bible says that if something makes you lose it—if it sparks a spirit of anger on the inside of you—the Bible says you are a *fool*, and you lack understanding.

It isn't just about you! Outbursts of anger injure other people. Understand that an outburst of anger injures other people, and internalized anger hurts the angry person!

Anger is diametrically opposed to love. Proverbs 15:1 says, "A soft answer turns away wrath, but a harsh word stirs up anger." I promise you will be tested on this! You will have to remember that a soft answer turns away anger. You might be in a conversation and someone starts going off on you, and you'll need to say, "Right now isn't a good time," or, "What we need to do is schedule an appointment." You might have to say, "Later on we can talk about this, because right now, I'm not going to be nice. Lets deal with this when the kids are asleep." A soft answer turns away anger.

The enemy wants to stir up anger—like a pot of soup. And nobody can make you angry like the people you love! When you open your heart up to them, they get a special anointing to make you mad! They can do it like no one else.

That's why husbands and wives go back and forth. That's why the husband says to the wife, "You are so silly; you can't do anything right!" You have to understand what is going on spiritually. The devil says to her, "Are you going to let him talk to you like that?" And then she says, "No, I'm not silly! You're the one that's silly!" Then the devil says to the man, "She disrespected you in your own house," so he says, "Look, woman, I'm the man in this house; you're not going to talk to me like that!"

The devil gets them going back and forth. In the midst of this, their innocent child walks in the room and asks to go outside, and they go off on the child! The spirit of anger now says to the child, "They are so mean to you! That's why you should never tell them what's going on in your life!" It's hard to remember that the Bible says, "A soft answer turns away wrath but harsh word stirs up anger" in these situations!

You have to learn through maturity how to deal with angry people—how to answer softly. When people are angry, they don't mean to be ugly and mean. You have to look at them and say, "Maybe he's in pain and dealing with some really difficult issues." That's another reason why you have to be careful of who you marry—you don't know what that person has been through. Most of the time, the thing couples argue about is not what's really at the source of their anger.

Proverbs 16:32 says, "He who is slow to anger is better than the mighty, and he who rules his spirit is better than he who takes a city." I know you preach, sing, usher, direct, and play, and I know you can pass out envelopes, but can you rule your spirit?

Unchecked anger acts as acid on the soul, and it eats away at your spirit and eventually destroys all feelings of love toward others.

Unchecked anger acts as acid on the soul, and it eats away at your spirit and eventually destroys all feelings of love toward others. Some people can't love at all because of bitterness and anger.

There has to be a difference in us as children of God, as opposed to those people who don't have a relationship with

Jesus Christ. We are the light of the world, cities on hillsides that cannot be hidden. We're the ones the Bible talks about— we're the light, the candle, that isn't put under a bushel but instead on a candlestick to give light to everyone!

The enemy's objective is to ruin your witness. it's hard for the unsaved to believe us anyway. They don't believe you have really changed! They think you are playing with God and with church. We must stop *trying* to convince them and start *being* who God has called us to be! Stop letting the enemy mess up your witness, goading you into doing something crazy so the people around you can say, "I told you that he didn't change!" The enemy will often use someone close to you.

When you understand your anger, you must neutralize it as soon as you are aware that you are experiencing it. If you don't neutralize your anger, you will repress it. Repressing anger is dangerous to you both physically and emotionally. When you do that, it's like burying anger alive—and it *will* erupt eventually. You try to pretend its not there, but there will be something that comes up that will cause it to come out of the grave. So don't suppress it or repress it!

Another mistake we make is expressing it. When anger is there all the time, you can't express it because generally you'll do so in a way that is hurtful or harmful to others. You can't go off every time something makes you angry.

You may be asking, "If I'm not supposed to suppress it or repress it or express it, what should I do?" The answer is in *confessing* it. Admit to God: "Lord, right now I am *angry*. I need You to give me some help and healing, because if You don't step in now, I'm going to make You and I look bad. I'm not going to act like its not here; I *am* upset! But I'm confessing it, Lord, because I need You to help me!

This is about maturity. We have to get to the point of confessing it. How many of you are saved and sanctified, and you're filled with the Holy Ghost, but you still get angry? A phone call can make you angry; an encounter at the job can make you angry; a thought can make you angry.

The devil knows when you open up to the spirit of anger, you are past the point where you can make good Godly decisions. Everything is distorted when you're angry, and don't forget: Anger is opposed to love. Anger will always make you find fault in someone else. You become very judgmental.

Anger is usually expressed in similar ways, and one of them is a physical or verbal outburst—saved or unsaved. Some of the least controlled individuals are in the body of Christ. They're Christians, and you don't have any idea what they're like when they're angry!

Church is not a good place—or at least the only place—to find a mate. What you have to understand is that when you see a person at church, they are at their very best. Most of the time, when you see them at church, they aren't behaving as they typically do. You say, "Oh, Lord, I just know this is the one for me!" He goes to church; she lifts her hands! Oh, Lord, I know he has to be the one! But how does he handle his anger? The average church is filled with actors and actresses.

It's not how you act in church but how you act when you get home. Do you lift your hands at home? Do you speak in tongues at home? Don't be fooled; if you are in church look-ing for someone other than the Lord Jesus, you will be sadly disappointed, because your church is the home of the Lord

Jesus Christ and not a dating institution. Church isn't where you come to get hooked up; the only person you need to get hooked up to is to Jesus! When you go to church, don't even look at anyone! (not literally . . .)

The devil is a liar. He will use whatever he can to pull you out of the will of God. Learn to wait on God. You have to understand, we all look good in church, but we *all* have something wrong with us! Let's understand what the church *really* is: It's not a museum for saints, it's a hospital for sinners. If we weren't sick, we wouldn't be in church! The only reason

You have to understand anger; you can't repress it, suppress it, or express it; you must confess it!

we are there is that we know our life's a mess, and we heard about a man named Jesus who is able to fix us up and turn us around! And a lot of us need a lot of help dealing with our anger!

So you have to understand anger; you can't repress it, suppress it, or express it; you must *confess* it! When anger is expressed in a wrong way, it is as a physical or verbal outburst. When a person is angry, that person may throw a punch, pound a fist against a wall; that person may slam a door or slam the phone; or he might swear or shout, or do a host of other physical manifestations.

Anger may even manifest itself as gossip. Gossipers attract other gossipers. Remember, the spirit of anger produces jealousy, and what do you think the source of gossip is? That's why there are some people who feast on every negative thing they find. They are in pain physically or emotionally. They are jealous. They want things their way.

Anger is expressed in two ways—as a physical outburst or as a brooding silence. The person who internalizes anger and allows it to seep into his subconscious will display his repressed anger as boredom or isolation from other people. The person who broods in silent anger may manifest an eruption of that anger at a later date, however. That brooding silence, that anger, may erupt in the body in the form of a disease. Unless one deals positively with anger, in a Godly manner, it will manifest itself in a negative way.

The Bible says that he who is slow to anger is better than the mighty, and a soft answer turns away wrath. The Bible also says that God got angry. Remember: "Be ye angry and sin not." Neither should you allow the sun to go down on your wrath.

Romans 12:18 says, "If it is possible, as much as depends on you, live peaceably with all men." He says put forth your greatest effort to live peaceably with all men. Look on to verse 19: "Beloved, do not avenge yourselves, but rather give place to wrath; for it is written, 'Vengeance is mine, I will repay,' says the Lord." He says, "I will repay." In other words, the Lord is saying, "Don't try to get back at your enemies!" He says, "Understand, vengeance is mine. I will repay." In verse 20, He says, "if your enemy is hungry, feed him; if your enemy is thirsty, give him drink; for in so doing, you will heap coals on his head." Finally, in verse 21 it says, "Do not be overcome by evil, but overcome evil with good. Put forth your best effort to live peaceably with all men—not angrily with all men."

Now pray this prayer with me:

"Father in the name of Jesus, I confess that I've had trouble in the past controlling my <u>anger</u>. I ask now that you would give me the strength to overcome this area of weakness. I boldly confess by the blood of Jesus that I'm free from being dominated by <u>anger</u>. No longer will the enemy cause my anger to provoke me to sin. In the name of Jesus, I'm free! Amen."

Don't repress your anger, suppress it, or express it; confess it, and live peaceably with all men, leaving vengeance to God.

CHAPTER THREE

JEALOUSY: GET OVER IT!

1 Samuel 18:5 reads:

So David went out wherever Saul sent him and behaved wisely. And Saul set him over the men of war, and he was accepted in the sight of all the people and also in the sight of Saul's servants. Now it happened when they were coming home, when David was returning from the slaughter of the Philistine, that the women had come out of all the cities of Israel, singing and dancing to meet King Saul, with tambourines, with joy, and with musical instruments. So the women sang as they danced and said: "Saul has slain his thousands, and David his ten thousands." Then Saul was very angry, and the saying displeased him; and he said, "They have ascribed to David ten thousand and to me only thousands. Now what more can he have but the kingdom?" So Saul eyed David from that day forward.

Saul eyed David from that day forward. I want to talk about overcoming the spirit of jealousy. You will see that this perhaps is the neighborhood in which many of us live. We talk about the visible sins of the flesh a lot in church, but there is one aspect of sin with which we hardly ever deal or discuss. It is hardly ever revealed, but this one sin is just as destructive as any of the other sins of the flesh. It is the sin of jealousy, which is attached to the sin of envy. Jealousy and envy hang out together. When jealousy is permitted, it produces envy; they go hand in hand.

Whether you know it or not, there is someone who is jealous of you—perhaps of what you have or how you look; perhaps of where you're headed; perhaps because of what you do. The truth of the matter is, there are people who are jealous of you. You need to know everybody who smiles at you is not necessarily your friend; not everyone who gets close to you just loves your company.

However, it doesn't matter who we are; we all at some point encounter a spirit of jealousy. Why doesn't anybody reveal it or talk about it? We all have a difficult time admitting that we are attacked by the spirit of jealousy, but it's time we learned to accept the fact that from time to time, we all experience jealousy. Instead of admitting it, however, we are stuck and say things like, "I'm just territorial," or, "I'm just possessive," or, "I'm just protecting what is mine." The truth is that jealousy is the problem.

Sometimes we cannot walk in obedience to God because we don't want anyone to talk about us. Did you know that they are talking about you anyway? Now that we are born again, as we grow up in Christ, we need to learn to overcome the flesh, and we need to become more secure in who we are in Christ. You have to get the attitude—without being arrogant or unforgiving—by saying, "Anyone who has a problem with me isn't my problem; it's their problem." Too many of us live our lives trying to please *people*. If people don't like you the way you are, tell them to take a hike. I'm not trying to be liked by jealous people.

"Player-haters" are not just in the world. The Church has "player-haters," also! There are possibly some jealous folk sitting back, preying on you because they don't want to see you make it—because *they* can't take it. Just wait until you get your breakthrough, and wait until you get where God wants you to be! Then you'll see some real jealousy! Tell yourself that you're going to succeed anyway; say, "I'm on my way!"

The Church is one of the best places to find the spirit of jealousy. Why can't we encourage others when God has blessed them instead of trying to put them down? The truth is that we need to get rid of the put-down mentality and say, "When God blesses one of His children, it doesn't matter what church he goes to or what denomination he belongs to; if it brings glory to God, then I'm *excited* about it!" Instead, in the Church we find one choir trying to out-sing another choir, or this preacher trying to out-preach that preacher. It's time for us to lay aside childish notions of gain! I feel that I need to reinforce that the Church is not exempt from jealously. Some of the biggest backbiters and gossipers sit in church pews!

Let me give you a definition for jealousy: to be jealous is to be hostile toward a rival or to someone you believe enjoys an advantage.

Some people are just *jealous*! They are jealous when God gives another person a gift or an ability. It appears that this person has an advantage, so now you feel inferior; the spirit of jealousy has just been born—one small seed of jealousy. Once that seed takes root in the soil of your soul, it can sprout overnight into a sprawling vine of envy. Now the choking tendrils of jealousy and envy can wind their way into every area of life!

When the spirit of jealousy is on the inside of you, it spreads its poison—an inflammation—as it grows so that your character becomes more and more tainted and distorted. You're not just jealous of the person you think has an advantage over you, you're downright envious; now you almost despise him and he hasn't bothered you!

But since it looks like he has an advantage over you, you envy him; because he drives what you want to drive and lives where you want to live, you're jealous; because he wears what you want to wear and has the ministry you want to have, you're jealous.

Be sensitive to the spirit of God and say, "Wait a minute! God, You're going to give me whatever you choose, regardless if someone else already has it or not! I'm going to be content with the blessings you give me!" When you understand what's yours is yours, you can rejoice when others get theirs!

Look at 1 Samuel 18:6. It says:

Now it happened when they were coming home, when David was returning from the slaughter of the Philistine, that the women had come out of all the cities of Israel, singing and dancing to meet King Saul, with tambourines, with joy, and with musical instruments. So the women sang as they danced and said: "Saul has slain his thousands, and David his ten thousands."

As the women danced and praised Saul, his head began to swell; then he heard the words, and all of the sudden he became very angry. The saying displeased him—that they ascribed ten thousands to David but only thousands to him. So now Saul is eying David from that day on, because Saul felt inferior to David. He was jealous.

You have to understand what was going on with Saul. All the girls were singing in the streets, and the soldiers were whistling the song while they walked in formation. Even the housewives hummed the song while washing the clothes and cooking dinner. Every time Saul heard the song, it was like smoke in his eyes and sand in his teeth.

Here is the question: What did David do wrong? He did absolutely nothing wrong! But now Saul is jealous of him, and soon he'll hate and despise David. Saul envied him, but David had done nothing wrong.

So watch what happens. Hatred and jealousy has welled up on the inside of this suspicious king. Saul said, "Wait a minute! What else can he do but take my throne?" What Saul did not understand was that the throne was *already* given. God told Saul to do one thing, and Saul did what many of us are guilty of doing: he modified the instructions of God; but simply because he hadn't vacated it yet, Saul didn't realize that his disobedience had cost him his throne. Just because you have the position doesn't mean you haven't already been fired! Although Saul had the position, God had already given David the power.

We need to take the Church back to where it needs to be. Everyone wants a position, but nobody wants the power. What good is the position if you don't have the power? Yes, you are standing in the pulpit, but are you living a holy life? Are you doing what God has instructed you to do? You can keep the position; I would rather have God give me the power! It's a horrible thing to be

> *Watch out for people who always find fault in someone else.*

fired by God and not know it. Fired! Suddenly you're in a position with no anointing, no power. And then you're jealous of anyone who does have power!

Hatred is welled up on the inside of Saul, so now his mind is working, constantly thinking of ways to destroy the young man everyone held in such high regard.

Jealousy can often lead a person to destroy another's life. Watch out for people who always find fault in someone else. There are some people you can get to talk about *anybody*. These people are so puffed up with pride that they can find fault with everyone else except themselves. The Church is sometimes responsible for shooting its wounded. The Church is sometimes the last place you can be real. The truth is, if it wasn't for His grace and mercy, we would all be on the fast track to hell. We have people in the Church with bad attitudes because of the spirit of jealousy. Your attitude can open or shut doors for you. You can be anointed or have money or have the ability, but a bad attitude—a spirit of jealousy—will keep you from getting the job, the raise, the loan, the vacation time.

Some people are just mean; they just want to cut everyone else. They have allowed the spirit of jealousy take root in their lives, and it's permanently planted. Your attitude creates a climate that either attracts people to you or causes them to dislike being around you. If people don't want to be around you, don't think it's because you are so spiritual; it could be because you are so hateful, that you're so possessed with envy and jealousy, that you're consumed. It could be that you are so heavenly bound that you are no earthly good!

I'm glad that I'm *God's* preacher; I'm not trying to preach for man's approval, God is saying right now, it's time for us to understand who we are. It's time we stopped pulling others down out of jealousy.

I have never forgotten what God showed me in a vision, though it has not come to pass yet. God showed me in a vision that I was in a huge stadium, and I saw myself preaching and saw another guy next to me interpreting because the people I was preaching to spoke another language. While I was preaching, the fellow next to me was interpreting. I remember in my vision that I looked around saw thousands of people. As I preached, I spoke and then paused, and the man next to me interpreted to the crowd.

I will never forget meeting a dear friend of mine. About a year and a half ago, He began to tell me about his ministry. He showed me some pictures of himself in a stadium, and he pointed to the man next to him and said, "This was my interpreter." He said that when he preached that night, over ten thousand souls came to the Lord. As we spoke—I didn't understand it or realize it at that point—but I began to say to myself, he can't preach like I preach. He doesn't have the charisma I have." I looked at the picture and thought, "Look at how he's dressed!"

Now, no one else heard me say that, but God heard me say it, and when I went back home, the spirit of the Lord spoke to me and said, "I will never do it for you because you are jealous." He said until I begin to appreciate what He was doing through someone else, He would never do it through me. All of a sudden it hit me, and I got down on my knees and began to cry and ask forgiveness. I had no idea I was even being jealous until the Lord brought it to my attention. He is my friend, and he is my brother—but I was jealous.

There are some of you reading this that have seen what God is doing in someone else's life but haven't praised God for what He's doing in them.

Understand that jealousy sneaks into our lives through different doors. Ladies, maybe there's a girl you know who is sharper than you. She is slim; she eats all she wants and never seems to get fat. You pick up weight by eating lettuce! So now you find yourself thinking, "I know she *has* to have a problem somewhere!" She looks good, but maybe she doesn't take care of her children. You think, "That dress looks all right, but look at her kids! The tree is known by its fruit!" Then you find out the sharp, slim lady keeps a good house and has well-behaved kids, and your mind keeps on working. So then you try reaching for something else. So you say, "She has a husband, but they aren't really in love."

Listen, jealousy filters through your pores as you try to find fault with other people. So here it is: in effect, the lady who wants to look like our slim woman with the well-behaved children and begins to despise her is actually guilty of *murdering* her; not with a gun or knife but with words and thoughts. God won't bless you until you get rid of jealousy!

Keep your head up, keep your shoulders back, and stay *humble*, because God has great things in store for you. He is going to give it to you and bless you in front of folks that don't like you—in front of people who can't get rid of their jealousy!

Let me tell you this, saints of God; understand that God has created us all the way He wants us to be. I have news for you—God's favor creates envy. When the favor of God is upon you, your enemies will begin to increase. There are some people who don't like you and have no idea why they don't like you; but *they* have to get over it! When God has placed favor on you, their jealousy isn't your problem; it's their problem!

The Bible says Saul looked at David—the Word says he "eyed him." Saul watched his every move. Why does your neighbor eye you? Because they see something that's in you, that's why! They can't figure out what it is, but there is something in you. They don't understand how you lost your job but still have joy. They are watching you, and if you've got God's favor, they're going to want it! This should bring us all to a greater place of obedience.

I know that I have enemies who wish I would fall. This causes me to be humble before God, to do the right thing so that the stuff I've done in the past stays in my past and isn't what I do now.

In 1 Samuel 18:10, it says:

And it happened on the next day that the distressing spirit from God came upon Saul, and he prophesied inside the house. So David played music with his hand, as at other times; but there was a spear in Saul's hand. And Saul cast the spear, for he said, "I will pin David to the wall!" But David escaped his presence twice.

You can eye me and hate me, but you can't catch me. Verse 12 says, "Now Saul was afraid of David, because the Lord was with him, but the Lord had departed from Saul." It's almost as though there was a transference; the Lord was once with Saul, but now He was somewhere else.

The Bible shows us that favor creates envy. You must be willing to pay the price for being highly favored, because when the favor of God is on you, there is a price.

The Bible says that Joseph was the favorite son, and his brothers envied him. They were going to kill him, but Rueben stopped them. He said, "We can't kill him; let's sell him." They threw him into a pit, sold him into slavery, and then he went to Potipher's house—went into the palace! The Bible says everywhere Joseph went, the Lord was with him.

You have to be willing to pay the price for being highly favored by God. David had to pay the price; Joseph had to pay the price; Jesus had to pay the price. The Bible says when they brought Jesus to crucify Him, the consensus was that they found no fault in Him. But He still had to go to the cross, because there is a price you have to pay when the favor of God is on you.

> *You have to be willing to pay the price for being highly favored by God.*

Some people don't like you, and don't know why they don't like you; could it be favor? Many of you are praying for money, but favor is better than money. Money can buy things, but the favor of God is infinitely better than money. Money can buy a house, but favor will get you approved despite bad credit; money can pay your bills, but the favor of God is His provision for *all* your needs.

The Spirit of the Lord spoke to me when I was flying from Long Beach, California about two years ago. I heard Him speak to me very clearly. He said, "Never speak another negative word concerning one of My servants." I know if it happened to me, it happens to others.

Begin to appreciate what people have to offer, because God has given us all different gifts, and just because I can't do what you can do doesn't mean I envy you. But I can appreciate the way God uses you. There is no patent pending on how God uses you or me. We need to learn to understand that God gives special gifts to special men and to appreciate the way God uses them.

James 3:14 says, "But if you have bitter envy and self-seeking in your hearts, do not boast and lie against the truth. This wisdom does not descend from above but is earthly, sensual, demonic." The Bible says if you have bitter envy and self-seeking in your own heart, that this type of wisdom does not come from above—it's earthly. It's sensual, and it's *demonic*. It's earthly, sensual, demonic wisdom when you can always find fault with everyone else but not yourself, when you are arrogant, puffed up, and prideful in your own heart.

Jealous people are motivated by fear and live a tormented life. Jealous people have a difficult time watching other people receive praise. Jealous people can't take it. Once jealousy comes into your life, everything changes. Your attitude changes, your demeanor changes; I believe even your health changes.

Saints, when you understand that God is not a respecter of persons, then and only then are you on the road to favor. Don't worry about what others are thinking or you will miss out on what God has. We need to appreciate what God is doing for others! That is the first step toward avoiding envy and jealousy.

Now let's pray concerning this subtle spirit:

"Father in the name of Jesus, I thank you that you know and understand everything about me. I confess that I've had problems concerning jealousy within my heart toward_____. Help me now to appreciate what you are doing in my brother's/sister's life, because I know every promise you made me concerning my future shall come to pass! Thank you in advance for this much needed deliverance, in the name of Jesus! Amen."

CHAPTER FOUR

THE GOD OF ANOTHER CHANCE

Isaiah 50:4 says:

> The Lord has given me the tongue of the learned, that
> I should know how to speak a word in season to him
> to that is weary. He awakens me morning by morning,
> He awakens my ear to hear as the learned.

I confess that this is my prayer as a modern-day messenger for the most high God—that He will give to me the
tongue of the learned, that I would not just speak a word but
always speak a word in season. There is nothing on earth
that compares to a word from God in season. If there is one
thing that I want to be guilty of, I want to be guilty of being
the type of pastor, preacher, teacher that always speaks his

words from God in season. I am sure that God has given me a word for this book, and I intend to cover this topic until the majority of God's people become not only hearers of the Word but doers, also.

I want to address how to overcome mistakes in this section of the book. Most of us don't have too far to look into our own personal lives to some mistakes for which we are perhaps still paying. Are you honest enough to admit that you've made mistakes since you've been saved? Would you be in the situation you're in now had you known back then what you know today?

The Word of God gives us instruction and insight for absolutely every area of our lives. I intend to go to the Word of God to get principles that will help us overcome the mistakes we've made in our lives.

Don't miss this principle. Your life is a result of your choices. Our lives are the sum total of the choices we've made. In that sense, your destiny, progress, and accomplishments—your ability to fulfill God's purpose for your life—is basically in your hands!

This is about overcoming your mistakes, because you're going to make them; this whole book is about overcoming various issues ranging from fear, rejection, to being in ruts. Many of you reading this are stuck taking a test—a test you've taken over and over again, and each time, you've made mistakes. You have failed, and God is giving you the same test in various forms over and over again.

First of all, let's figure out what a mistake really is. By way of definition, a mistake is misunderstanding the meaning or intention of a thing, or a person; it's a wrong judgment on character. It's simply being wrong—making an incorrect judgment, a wrong call, missing it, blowing it. Personal discipline, is one of the things that so many of us lack. I want you to understand that whatever you fail to master in your life can eventually master you—whatever it is. Whether it's anger, an addiction, or an attitude, if you fail to deal with it—if you make mistakes in getting it out of your life—it will eventually deal with you. Many of you may only be dealing with an attitude that God wants to adjust, but don't think you can skip reading this because you're not addicted to alcohol or aren't dealing with a spirit of anger. Some of you messed up when you picked up this book, because God will hold you responsible for what you've received here.

God will bring issues to the surface in our lives over and over until we get the victory over them. For instance, some of you have dealt with fear all of your life; you've been fearful about something since you were a little child.

When I was in the military, I was forced to deal with a fear of heights. One day, the Spirit of God said, "Here you are preaching My gospel, telling people how good I am; but when are you going to conquer fear?" I said I had already conquered

> *If you fail a test with God, He won't let you progress until you pass it—you'll take it over and over.*

it. I remember going through an obstacle course in boot camp, and we had to climb up this tower and then down. I got to the top, and I couldn't let my partners know that I was scared to death—especially when I looked down.

LOOK TO THE HILLS . . .

Going over the edge was one of the hardest things I'd ever done; however, when I came down, my fear of heights was broken. I finally conquered the fear of heights.

What kinds of things in your life are dominating you—things you know have a hold on you that you've never dealt with? I've learned that if you fail a test with God, He won't let you progress until you pass it—you'll take it over and over.

Are you tired of making mistakes? They cost you severely. Let me show you a principle here. Luke 5:1-11 says:

> So it was, as the multitude pressed about Him to hear the word of God that He stood by the Lake of Gennesaret, and saw two boats standing by the lake; but the fisherman had gone from them and were washing their nets. Then He got into one of the boats, which was Simon's, and asked him to put out a little from the land. And He sat down and taught the multitudes from the boat. When He had stopped speaking, He said to Simon, "Launch out into the deep and let down your nets for a catch." But Simon answered Him and said to Him, "Master, we have toiled all the night and we have taken nothing; nevertheless, at Your word, I will let down the net." And when they had done this, they caught a great number of fish, and their net was breaking. And they signaled to their partners in the other boat to come and help them. And they came and filled both the boats so that they began to sink. When Simon Peter saw it, he fell down at Jesus' knees, saying, "Depart from me, for I am a sinful man, O Lord!" For he and all who were with him were astonished at the catch of fish

54

which they had taken; and so also were James and John, the sons of Zebedee, who were partners with Simon. And Jesus said to Simon, "Do not be afraid. From now on you will catch men." So when they had brought their boats to the land, they forsook all and followed Him.

These individuals who were privileged to be called His disciples often seem to us to be larger than life. On the contrary, I want you to understand that these disciples of Christ were very much alike to you and me. Simon Peter is a great example, because he can pass a test with an A one minute and an F the next—on the same test. Very much like all of us!

When I look at this text, I see two people: Peter and Jesus. Both were fishing, but they were fishing for different things—Peter for fish, Jesus for followers. Peter's eyes were on the physical, the natural, but Jesus was paying attention to the spiritual. Jesus very simply invites Peter to get involved in the same things in which He is involved; that's what Jesus does for us. He comes into our lives and gets us involved in that which He's involved. In other words, Jesus was asking Peter to lay aside his agenda and take up His instead; He asked Peter to get his eyes off the physical to see what He sees in the spiritual.

Here is the interesting part. If you lay aside your agenda, if you see to the spiritual first, He will meet your physical needs later. Many of us can't get what God wants us to have because we aren't willing to lay aside our agenda and pick up His; but He says, "If you go after the spiritual, I'll give you the physical later." We want the physical now, though! We don't want to suffer for the sake of God's name. We want it quick, now! We're in a hurry!

Jesus is telling you that you need to get into what's important to Him. Then He'll grant you what you've been asking for—the physical after the spiritual. Most of the time, when you find yourself stuck in a rut, you're in a situation God never intended you to be in, because the spiritual needs to come first!

Matthew 6:33 tells us to "seek the kingdom of God and His righteousness first, and that all the other things will be added—later." Are you with me? Seek first the kingdom of God and His righteousness—spiritual—and all these other things will be added to you—physical. That's the way it is.

Malachi 3:10 says:

Bring all the tithes into the storehouse [spiritual—tithe], that there may be food in My house, and try Me now in this, says the Lord of hosts, if I will not open for you the windows of heaven and pour out for you such blessing that there will not be room enough to receive it [physical—blessings].

2 Chronicles 7:14 says:

If My people, who are called by My name, will humble themselves and pray and seek My face and turn from their wicked ways [spiritual], then I will hear from heaven and will forgive their sin and heal their land [physical].

God is telling us that if we get involved in the spiritual, He'll take care of the physical! He says that the blessings are yours, but your priorities are out of order. He is asking you to give Him what He wants so He can give you what you want and need! He won't give it to you if you're doing your own thing. He's telling us to put ourselves in the background. If you want to follow Him, you've got to deny yourself, take up His cross, and follow Him; but many of us want it *now*. We don't want to go through the proper channels. However, when you get desperate for God's blessing, you'll take it any way you can get it.

Man will often try to counterfeit what God originates, and one of the worst things you can do is go through a door opened to you by man. If man opens the door for you, when man gets mad at you, he'll slam the door. However, when God opens a door for you, there's

> *When God opens a door for you, there's nothing man can do but watch your back as you go through the door.*

nothing man can do but watch your back as you go through the door.

Let's go back to our text in Luke. Remember, Jesus is saying to us that He'll give us what we want if we'll give Him what He wants. In verse four, Jesus makes a request: He asks Peter to go out into the deeper water and to let down his nets. He knows what Peter is looking for. Jesus makes a request, and Peter responds—even though they had labored all night and hadn't caught anything, he does it because Jesus asks it of him.

Pay attention to what Jesus asks Peter, because it's what He's asking of many of us: He asks us to launch out into the deep—because, Peter, what God has for you, you can't receive in shallow water. To get what God has for you, Peter, you'll have to push off from shore—where you are; go out into the deep, where God wants you to be. If you stay where you are, Peter, and don't go where He asks, what He intends will never happen, because what He wants to do for you is so big that shallow water can't contain it.

One of our problems is that we're in relationships with shallow folk. We're hanging around with shallow people, doing shallow things. But what God wants for you can't hap-

> *What God wants for you can't happen in the shallow places; it has to be out in the deep, where you've never been before.*

pen in the shallow places; it has to be out in the deep, where you've never been before. In order to get what you've never had before, you've got to be willing to do what you've never done before!

God wants you to launch out into the deep. Because what He's got for you isn't a thirty-fold blessing; it's not a sixty-fold blessing—that's not where you're supposed to be living. He wants to give you a hundred-fold blessing! He wants to bless you in such a way that everyone who sees it will know it was God!

Are you willing to push off? Are you ready to leave some people behind, to cut off some shallow relationships, and shallow ties?

Can you imagine what Peter is thinking in the natural while Jesus is asking him to push off? He tells Jesus that they've been fishing all night, and he's been a fisherman all his life. I can almost here him reminding Jesus of that: "Now

Jesus, I'm a fisherman and You're a carpenter. I've never come down to your carpenter shop and tried telling you how to hammer a nail, right? And you're telling me how to fish?"

But I can hear Jesus' response: "Peter, I know that you've been fishing all your life; I know you've got a degree in "fishology;" you've got ships and all that. But Peter, it looks to me that despite all that, you've got everything but fish." And Peter says, "Okay, just because it's You, Jesus, I'll let the net down." He launches out.

Peter reminds Jesus that they've been fishing all night and haven't caught anything; your past can prevent your progress, also. Jesus is seeking to bless Peter, and Peter just brings up the past. Many of us are stuck in our past; we're holding on to stuff that God wants us to release; He wants us to push off from shore. It's time to let go.

There is another interesting detail I'd like to point out. The Bible tells us that after they push off and they've got their great number of fish, their net breaks. Wait a minute! Who is "they?" We were talking about Peter and Jesus, right? "They" are the other people in the boat with Peter, and it illustrates that what God has for you isn't just for you! It's for everyone around you; everyone you're influencing. There's a man reading this that doesn't understand he's holding back his whole family; there is a business owner that doesn't know she's been keeping her business and her employees back. When we step out, we often take those near us along into the blessing!

We form preconceived notions of how the Lord is going to bless us, but God wants to give you so much, you won't have room enough to contain it; your nets will break and you'll have to have help in order to bring home what He wants to give you.

Obey God totally; if you've got more than one net and He tells you to launch out and drop your nets, drop them all! Don't hold back because you've been toiling all night. God tells us to bring our tithe and offering into the store-house, but are you picking one? If the devil can't get you to disobey God totally, he'll get you to disobey partially—to compromise.

When we step out, we often take those near us along into blessing!

Peter's past intruded on his progress, and he didn't practice his principles perfectly; in addition, his pattern prohibited his prosperity. Peter let down a net—not all his nets, one net—and instead of getting all the fish that Jesus called for him, some got away to be caught by others another day. Are your blessings slipping away because you only partially obey?

Many of us are in pain because of our decisions. But there's no one else to blame. Our pain is discomfort created by disorder; disorder created by our decisions, our failures, and our mistakes—our partial obedience. Pain is not our enemy, however—it's an indicator. Pain is the messenger that tells you your real enemy is out there, that the devil is in the neighborhood. Paying attention to what gives you pain can save you from a life of disasters. Pay attention to your mistakes!

As a child, did you ever touch a hot iron? It hurt, didn't it? The pain made you jerk your hand away. If you would not have experienced the pain, you would not have withdrawn your hand quickly, and you could have experienced greater injury.Praise God for the pain you've experienced!

Having said all that, I still have not directly discussed how to overcome your mistakes. Luke 5:8 tells us. What does Peter do when he sees the miracle? He falls down at Jesus' feet and recognizes that he isn't worthy of what God did for him.

How do you overcome your mistakes? The first step is recognizing them. You *must* recognize that you've made the mistake. It might have looked good at first, but what looks good isn't always God. However, often we can't—or refuse to—recognize that we've made a mistake; the devil has us totally out of position.

Second, you must admit—out loud—that you've missed it; you must call it what it is. If it's sin, call

> *The closer you get to Jesus, the more you will see your own faults.*

it sin. Verbalize it. Many of us recognize our mistakes, but we don't confess them. Peter fell down at Jesus' feet, and he verbalized it: "Depart from me, for I am a sinful man, O Lord!" This is one reason I really like Peter; he blew it, but he is real, and he confronts it.

The closer you get to Jesus, the more you will see your own faults. Too often in the Church, we see others' faults but not our own. When you really get close to Jesus, you'll find out that you don't have time to be talking about what anyone else is doing because you see too much of what's going on in your own life. People without mercy are people who are far from Jesus, because otherwise they'd recognize their own need for grace and they would be easier on others.

61

So in order to deal with your mistakes, you must first recognize that you've made them. Then verbalize your mistakes; confess them. The key, however, is getting close to Jesus. A little time with Jesus will take care of everything! Be willing to launch out into the deep, because it is there, away from the

> *A little time with Jesus will take care of everything!*

shallow things in your life— your friends, your own agenda—where God gives you what He's got in store for your life. Pay attention to the spiritual, and then He will bless you with the physical. Yet don't try to counterfeit God's blessings. Put Him first, and He will make sure you get what you need!

So push out and lower your nets! And don't hold back, don't make the same mistake you've made before and only drop one net because you're tired. Drop them all, and He will give you blessings that you cannot contain, and they will affect not only you but also your whole family!

Now let's pray:

"Father in the name of Jesus, I thank you for being a God of another chance. Lord you are well aware of the mistakes I've made in my life by only giving you partial obedience. Please forgive me for every mistake I've made that has paralyzed my progress. I receive your forgiveness, and thank you for giving me a fresh start in Jesus name! Amen."

CHAPTER FIVE

LIVE, FORGIVE, GIVE

At this point, let us discuss how we can overcome rejection. You will be surprised at how many people look good on the outside, but a lot is happening on the inside. The devil is tormenting them in their minds, and I know without doubt that there are people reading this today who know first-hand what it is like to experience significant rejection.

2 Kings 7:3 says:

> There were four leprous men at the entrance of the gate; and they said to one another, "Why are we sitting here until we die? If we say, 'We will enter the city,' the famine is in the city, and we shall die there. And if we sit here, we die also. Now therefore, come, let us surrender to the army of the Syrians. If they

keep us alive, we shall live; and if they kill us, we shall
only die." And they arose at twilight to go to the camp
of the Syrians; and when they had come to the outskirts of the Syrian camp, to their surprise no one was
there. For the Lord had caused the army of the
Syrians to hear the noise of chariots and the noise of
horses—the noise of a great army; so they said to one
another, "Look, the king of Israel has hired against us
the kings of the Hittites and the kings of the Egyptians
to attack us!" Therefore, they arose and fled at twilight
and left the camp intact—their tents, their horses and
their donkeys—and they fled for their lives. And when
these lepers came to the outskirts of the camp, they
went into one tent and ate and drank, and carried
from it silver and gold and clothing, and went back
and hid them; then they came back and entered
another tent, and carried some from there also and
went and hid it. They said to one another, "We are
not doing right. This day is a day of good news, and
we remain silent. If we wait until morning light, some
punishment will come upon us. Now therefore, come,
let us go and tell the king's household." So they went
and called to the gatekeepers of the city and told
them, saying, "We went to the Syrian camp, and sur-
prisingly no one was there, not a human sound—only
horses and donkeys tied and tents intact."

We all have experienced rejection in some form. My
assignment from God in this portion of the book is to teach
you—to show you by Biblical principles—how to overcome

rejection, and we're going to start by learning lessons from these lepers.

Now if you ever saw a group of individuals who were expecting to die, it was these four men; they were lepers. Now understand that in Biblical times, leprosy was the most dreaded, embarrassing, ostracizing disease that existed. It was a terrible thing to be diagnosed with the disease of leprosy. These individuals experienced rejection *everywhere* they went.

There was a famine in the land. It was such a terrible famine that the Bible says there was no food *anywhere*. There were many people in desperate need of food, the Bible says they began to eat one another! Now that is a serious famine! 2 Kings 6 even tells us a story about two women that decide they were going to eat their *children!*

In the midst of this great terrible famine, these four men who were not only starving, but keep in mind they've also been diagnosed with this dreadful disease, leprosy. Let me help you to understand the laws of the day. In Numbers 5:1, the Bible says:

> And the Lord spoke to Moses, saying: "Command the children of Israel that they put out of the camp every leper, everyone who has a discharge, and whoever becomes defiled by a corpse. You shall put out both male and female; you shall put them outside the camp, that they may not defile their camps in the midst of which I dwell." And the children of Israel did so, and put them outside the camp; as the Lord spoke to Moses, so the children of Israel did.

LOOK TO THE HILLS . . .

I'm trying to set the stage and show you that these individuals experienced incredible rejection everywhere they went. They were rejected by society because they had this dreadful disease. The Bible tells us they were put out because God said so! These individuals knew rejection first hand. In Leviticus 13:44 the Bible says:

> He is a leprous man. He is unclean. The priest shall surely pronounce him unclean; his sore is on his head. Now the leper on whom the sore is, his clothes shall be torn and his head bare; and he shall cover his mustache and shall cry, "Unclean! Unclean!" He shall be unclean. All the days he has the sore he shall be unclean. He is unclean, and he shall dwell alone; his dwelling shall be outside the camp.

The Bible says that because they were lepers, they had to shout, "Unclean! Unclean!" If they were approaching a group of individuals—if they had leprosy, they had to warn everyone that they were coming and cry out, "Unclean! Unclean!" Imagine that; everywhere they went, they were shunned. People scattered as they got near. These four men experienced *rejection*!

There were times when they would draw a circle, and those with leprosy were commanded to live within that circle! The only people that brought them food were close relatives, because no one else wanted to have anything to do with them. People looked at these lepers and thought, "I wish they would hurry up and die! Look how ugly they are—sores all over their bodies." They were rejected because of their sickness; they were rejected because of their disease; they were rejected because of their condition.

Understand the point: All of us alive today, will have some type of condition. We all have something in our lives that we wish we didn't have. I don't know if you know this, but you are sitting next to a leper! You work with them every day; you might even live with one!

We all have experienced what it's like to be rejected. Some of us have been rejected because of our shape. You may have been rejected because of your color. You might have been rejected because you lack education, or because you have a big nose or big lips. You may have been rejected because you don't have money, or perhaps because you can't speak well. You may have been rejected because you were once addicted to drugs. You may have been rejected because you had a baby out of wedlock, or you may have been rejected because you had an abortion. Maybe you were rejected because your family looked at you with great expectations, but you let them down. We *all* have been rejected! You've been rejected for a job; you've been turned down for credit; you've been rejected for a relationship. We all experience rejection.

It's time to get over it. God wants to show us from His Word how to overcome rejection. "This is your season."

Let's go back to 2 Kings 7:3. There were four leprous men who sat at the entrance of the gate. They talked to each other and wondered why they were just sitting there, waiting to die. They said among themselves, "What are we doing just sitting here?"

If you are going to overcome rejection you must be committed to living. Are you determined to live? You have to make up your mind that you are *determined* to live. Some of you have gone through problems since you were a child, but if you are going to overcome rejection, you have to be committed to living.

The lepers said, "Why are we just sitting here? If we sit here we are going to die." They figured if they entered the city, they would die because of the famine. However, if they sat where they were, they knew they would die, also. So they thought, "What about surrendering to the Syrian army?" If the Syrians showed them mercy, they would live—at least for a while—but if they killed them, it wouldn't be too big of a deal; they were going to die anyway.

They had four choices. First of all, they said they could stay right where they were—they knew that if they waited long enough, they would die. Their second choice was attempting to go back into the city, but there was a famine on, and they knew they would die there, too. Their third choice was eating each other, but then three of them at least would probably die. However, their fourth choice was attempting to get into the enemy's camp. They figured, "If they capture us and we become prisoners, we'll still be alive. But if we die, what's the big deal? We're going to die anyway!"

We must learn a lesson from these lepers and make up in our minds, "I am *committed* to living." You might not be able to change your skin—your condition of leprosy—but you can change your attitude, your mental condition.

The problem with many of us is that we're waiting to get in heaven what God wants us to have right now. God says that you don't have to wait to get to heaven to have peace; you can have peace right now! You don't have to wait to get to heaven to have joy; you can have joy right now!

The devil has the cards stacked against you, but God wants you to know that it's time to live—because if you stay sitting where you're sitting, you are *going* to die. God is saying that it's time to get up; it's time to *move!* If you are going to get back your groove, you've got to bust a move. God is saying that it's time to take yourself out to dinner; ladies get your hair done; get your nails done. Say to yourself, "He walked out on me; it's over, but I'm going to live!" Don't sit there moaning and complaining. It wasn't your loss! It was *his* loss!

> *The devil has the cards stacked against you, but God wants you to know that it's time to live.*

It's not over till God says it's over. If I have Jesus, He can give me what money can't buy. The problem with many of us is we are standing still. God is saying to someone, that you need to get back in school; you need to find another job! Stop walking around in house slippers and your robe, waiting for someone to knock on your door and give you a job. Dress up, get out, and tell yourself, "I'm going to be somebody!" Stop hanging with zeros. If your hanging with zeros, you will never be a hero. It's time to hang around folks who are going somewhere!

Tell yourself it's time to live, that it's time to get up. These four men said, "Wait a minute! If we sit here, we'll die."

71

They had the attitude: we don't have anything to lose. They said, "We are going to the Syrians, and if they catch us and make us slaves, at least we will be alive! But if they kill us, it's not a big deal; we're going to die anyway." However, when they go to the camp, no one was there. They got to the outskirts of the camp, and they didn't hear anything. They probably said to themselves, "Wait a minute; this is the enemy's camp, right? So where are the enemies?"

God caused the army of the Syrians to hear the noise of chariots and the noise of horses—the noises of a great army. They thought that the king of Israel hired a bunch of Hittites and Egyptians to attack them, so as the four lepers were coming at twilight, the Syrians were fleeing leaving their camp intact. They left their tents, horses, and their donkeys, and they ran for their lives! The Lord made the eight legs of four leprous men sound like forty million, and it was just four lepers walking; but the enemy heard them coming and thought it was an army, and they *ran*! God wants you to know that if you would just get up and take Him at His Word, He'd take care of your enemies!

When the lepers came into the first tent, the first thing they did was to get something to eat and drink. However, they also got gold, silver, and clothes; everything that once belonged to the enemy now belonged to them, and they didn't

If you are going to overcome rejection, you have to be committed to living.

have to do anything but step out in faith! Do you know that the wealth of the wicked is laid up for the righteous? God takes money out of the hands of heathens, and He puts it in the hands of His people. If you are going to overcome rejection, you have to be committed to living.

Secondly, if you are going to overcome rejection, you've got to be committed to forgiving. Many of us want to live, but many of us don't want to forgive. The story goes on to say that they agreed they weren't doing right by keeping quiet about the good news—that the Syrians had fled—and they figured that if they waited until morning, some punishment would come upon them. So they decided to go tell the king. In other words, they decided to share all that they had found with the king and his household.

Wait a minute! Did they forget that it was the king and the others in the city that had rejected them? They understood that in order to not lose their blessing, they needed to bless someone else. And whom did they decide to bless? The same ones that kicked them out of the city!

God says that the first thing you've got to do in order to get ready for what He has for you is to forgive! Fathers, forgive your children; workers, forgive your bosses; women, forgive the men that misused you.

In order for you to be blessed, you've got to forgive, and it's not easy; that's for sure! However, there isn't anyone—or anything—worth getting your blessings cut off over. You're worried about the child support you have never received, but God will take care of you and your children; He'll bless you, but you have to forgive. Let it go.

We often cannot move on because we are holding on to stuff that is keeping us back. If you regard iniquity in your heart, you're blocking God's answer to your prayers.

Forget the people who fired you even though you didn't do anything wrong. You've got to be willing to forgive. If God shut a door, He will open another door better than the last!

The first thing you have to do is bust a move—decide to live, and get up and moving! Dry your eyes and quit complaining about what you don't have; it's time to live. After you decide to live, you've got to forgive. We'll get more into for-

> *If you are going to overcome rejection, you have to be committed to forgiving.*

giveness later, but for now, understand that forgiveness is the second step to overcoming rejection.

I'm sure that issues are being broken in your life as you read this book. Some of you picked up this book feeling rejected, but I want you to know that what God has for you is for *you*; no one can stop you from getting what God has for you—no one but you! You have stepped over—into destiny. The devil will regret the day you picked up this book and read these life changing principles, because now you're committed to live!

Being committed to living is logical, but being committed to forgiving is radical! If you don't want to block the blessings God has for you, you've got to forgive those that hurt you—bless them! The Word says they went and said to the king, "We have to bless you, king."

Not only do you have to be committed to living, and forgiving, you have to be committed to giving. Some of you might be thinking that it doesn't make sense; why bless the ones that rejected you? You might be saying that it doesn't make sense. I say it makes a lot of sense! You have to look back over what you've been through and thank God for even your enemies. They didn't kill you; they blessed you. They didn't really hurt you; they actually helped you. Because, if you didn't have so many enemies, you

Being committed to living is logical, but being committed to forgiving is radical!

probably wouldn't be worshipping God, and you might not know how much you need God!

Take Joseph as an example. His brothers sold him into slavery. They threw him into a pit! But the Bible says that Joseph looked at the same people that hurt him and said, "What you meant for evil, God meant for good."

When you look back over your life, you're going to see that the enemy is not very clever, because if he would have left you alone, some of you may not be saved today. But the devil just doesn't understand that the more he tries you, the more you're going to give God praise.

Instead of complaining about everything you've been through, stop and say, "Lord, thank you! Thank you for the people that smiled in my face while stabbing me in the back. Thank you for the people who aren't any good for me!" Because I've got news for you: When God blesses you, He will bless you in front of your enemies! Give God praise for the hell that you've been through! God is ready to open a door for you even as you read this. Go into the enemy's camp where you can get your stuff, your blessing! God is going to give you everything the devil has stolen from you. Receive peace! Receive joy! I want my family back! Receive restoration in your family. It's time to get everything that belongs to you!

No weapon formed against you is going to prosper! The enemy wants to keep you from walking in Destiny.

It is time for you to live; it's time for you to forgive; and it's time for you to start giving. I have a Godly confidence that as you read this, everything in your life is about to break free! It's time to go into the enemy's camp to get your stuff. You've may have been through hell,

> *When God blesses you, He will bless you in front of your enemies!*

but you're not going to sit there and die, are you? You're not going to go out sitting down! Say to yourself, "I'm going to get up!" You are an overcomer!

Right now, the enemy is confused. He has hit you with his best shot, and you're coming right back up. He's not going to keep you down, rejected. You're going to overcome it, because greater is He that is in you than he that's in the world!

Thank you Jesus! You might not know how it's going to happen, but it starts when you get up and decide to live, forgive, and give! In the long run, the people you thought hurt you actually helped you. If you had not gotten rejected, you never would have gotten back up; and then you wouldn't have learned anything.

God made the four leprous men sound like a whole army! I love the fact that the enemy ran off and left all of his stuff; and guess who all that stuff belonged to? Sinful man.

One last thing: in this text, they did everything together. "Us" is actually "we." I don't want God to only bless me—or just you. Take

> *You might not know how it's going to happen, but it starts when you get up and decide to live, forgive, and give!*

somebody with you, and get up from where you are!

Let's pray:

"Father in the name of Jesus, I thank you for revealing to me that I am not what they call me, I'm only what I answer to, and I realize that I am the righteousness of God created in Christ Jesus. Thank you for setting me free from the spirit of rejection. The victory is mine. I will lift mine eyes to the hill . . . in Jesus' name! Amen."

CHAPTER SIX

DON'T CUT OFF YOUR BLESSINGS

In this section, I will address unforgiveness. To begin, we are going to examine Mark 11:24-26, in which Jesus discusses forgiveness as He says:

> Therefore I say to you, whatever things you ask when you pray, believe that you receive them, and you shall have them. And whenever you stand praying, if you have anything against anyone, forgive him, that your Father in heaven may also forgive you your trespasses. But if you do not forgive, neither will your Father in heaven forgive you.

Jesus begins by discussing faith—that whatever you ask and believe, you'll receive. As what you want lines up

79

with His Word, if you have the faith to believe for it, it's yours. However, the condition is that if you don't forgive, your heavenly Father will not forgive you. It seems simple, but it's very powerful!

Jesus tells us that our faith can get us the blessings of God—but that only one thing can stop you from receiving the desires of your heart, unforgiveness.

All of us have been hurt. We've all been disappointed and let down. I guarantee that at some point in life you've failed to forgive—even if it's a minor thing. Lack of forgiveness will hold you back. When we really think about it, we didn't deserve to be forgiven, but God still forgave us. The way God forgave us is no different than the way we are also called to forgive others, even when they do not deserve to be forgiven.

Some of you may agree, but others are saying, "But you don't know what she said to me!" or, "But you don't understand how many times he's let me down and failed me!" In saying that, you're perfectly correct: I don't understand. However, what I do understand is that God is simply saying to you that the only thing keeping you from getting what you ask of Him is unforgiveness.

Some of you are going through difficult times—your lives are looking very negative—but while you're thinking it's the enemy, it is actually a harvest that you have planted. God is telling you quite plainly that you can cry, you can fast, and you can make circles on your knees as you pray. But if there is unforgiveness in your heart, God says He's not hearing your supplications.

There are Christians with titles and positions in our churches who shout, dance and sing, but they can't get a breakthrough for their prayers; God is saying it's because the line is clogged up. God is trying to get through to us that He forgave us after all we've done to Him, and He won't open the floodgates until we get rid of our grudges and forgive those that have hurt us!

God has brought me to a conclusion: no one is worth getting my blessings being cut off. I need too much help and too many blessings from God, to walk around holding grudges against the people who have harmed me. I don't care how difficult it is to let go of the wrongs that have been done to me; nothing is as difficult as living behind the walls of unforgiveness. When you fail to forgive, you put up walls; you think you're free, but you're in a prison. You're bound, living behind the walls of unforgiveness.

What does it mean to forgive? To understand unforgiveness, we have to understand what it means to forgive. You know you've really forgiven someone when it doesn't hurt anymore; it means you can see them, hear them and work right next to them, and though you remember what they did—you're wiser for it—the pain of what they did is gone, it's behind you.

So in a sense, forgiving means that you've ceased to feel resentment. So what then is unforgiveness? Unforgiveness is when you are unwilling or unable to forgive. Those who don't forgive, are in one of two areas: either they refuse to let go and forgive, or they don't know how. Some of us are unwilling, and others are unable.

Many of Jesus' teachings are on building and maintaining relationships with God and man. He first teaches us how to build a relationship with God, and then He teaches us how to build a relationship with our fellow men. Jesus taught relationship. And though our relationship with God is paramount—a relationship that Jesus' death on the cross restored—we cannot survive without relationships to our fellow men. God has to be our highest priority—not money or our husbands or the wives or possessions, not the degree we have earned, and not the position we have attained.

Our understanding of who God is—our relationship—will determine how we get through things and how long it takes. You see, God is not like man; if He makes a promise, He's going to keep it. If you didn't understand that about God, you might have given up a long time ago; you might have turned your back. Instead, something inside lets you know that your blessing is close; you have faith. It might look silly to those around you, but you know you're almost there; you may not know what job you'll have next week, but you know you're almost there; you don't have a husband or wife, but you have a promise! The promise is that if you seek God first, and His righteousness, then all the other things will be added to you! Tell yourself, "I'm almost there."

Some of you might feel that you are not in a place where you feel this section is for you; read it anyway. This chapter is directed at those of you who are going through hell right now; those of you who seem to be suffering every time you turn around. Adversity is the enemy's reaction to your progress.

But all of that is a side issue. Jesus wants you to know that He isn't only interested in your relationship with Him—

82

although that is by far your most important relationship. Our relationship with God should produce within us a quality such as—character—that builds and sustains all of our relationships.

Here's where I'm going with this: the more I learn about God and the closer I get to Him, the more mercy I have for others and the easier it is to forgive.

Adversity is the enemy's reaction to your progress.

People who don't forgive have not come to truly understand what God has done for them and how merciful He is. The truth of the matter is that you aren't the recipient of His grace, favor and blessings because you're good or haven't broken His commandments. You have a restored relationship with God because of His grace and His mercy.

Unforgiveness holds you hostage; it makes you a prisoner. Any time you don't forgive, you build a wall of pain around your life.

Unforgiveness is selfishness. Show me a Christian man and woman who can't make their marriage work, and I'll show you possibly two selfish people. Selfishness is the destroyer of two out of three marriages—not lost love. Jesus said that if you want to be one of His disciples, you have to deny yourself and pick up His cross and follow Him. You have to lay aside your own agenda, and that includes the bitterness you might hold for those that have hurt you.

I'm not saying that it is easy—it's not easy to be a follower of Christ—but I am saying that if you pray and ask God for strength to forgive, you'll help to free yourself and the blessings He's got in store for you.

When we do not forgive, it is because we're not willing to let go of our wounded pride and admit that we're hurt. When we get hurt, when our pride gets damaged, we don't like to admit it, and we get angry instead. The truth is you're not really angry, you're hurt. But we don't like to admit it.

> *Unforgiveness holds you hostage; it makes you a prisoner.*

It's an even bigger blow to our wounded pride to admit that someone else's action actually injured us. It shows that we're vulnerable, that we're not in complete control; that maybe we haven't got it all together. We hide behind our anger.

Unforgiveness is you hiding behind your anger—we use it to cover our wounded pride. It's okay to hurt; It happens to everyone. You're not unusual, and what he did to you, what she did to you, isn't unique to the history of mankind.

Let me show you something powerful. Psalm 66:18 says: "If I regard iniquity in my heart, the Lord will not hear." The Greek translation says: if you regard iniquity in your heart, the Lord isn't going to hear. Want it in Hebrew? It means that if you regard iniquity in your heart, the Lord isn't going to hear you. If you don't forgive, God does not listen to you.

Those who do not forgive don't want to let go of the pain. They wear it like a badge. What righteous indignation, what hurt, what individual is worth losing your blessings over? If you hold onto it—no matter how justified you think you are—you're nullifying your prayers by entertaining sin: the sin of unforgiveness.

Do you think it's possible you can't get your breakthrough because God isn't going to give it to you until you

84

prove you have the maturity to let go of your grudges? Whoever hurt you, let it—and them—go! If you don't forgive them, God can't forgive you.

Let's take a forgiveness test. The answer is either going to be "yes," or it's going to be "no"—there are no "maybes." You have to be honest with yourself.

- Are you continually thinking and rehearsing something that someone did to you?
- Do you feel anger or resentment toward anyone regularly?
- Is there anyone that you purposefully avoid or do not communicate with?

If you answered "yes" to any of these questions, the first thing you need to do is ask the Lord to forgive you for holding onto unforgiveness. Next, you have to consciously ask Him to help you forgive the other person. Now say to yourself, "It hurt me, but it really helped me." See, if you weren't hurting, you may not be looking for God; you may not have had to turn to Him. The bad thing that happened to you can work for good because it turns you to God and teaches you something.

But here's the deal: it's not bad when you have to take a test; it's bad when you have to take the same test over and over. Keep in mind, though, that even failing doesn't make you a failure—quitting makes you a failure.

For God to forgive your trespasses, you must forgive those that hurt you. Christians in the average church are doing nothing but spiritual aerobics: they're crying and shouting and speaking in tongues, but they're not going anywhere. God isn't moved by your actions—He's looking at your heart. We can fool one another, but we can't fool God.

You've been there and done that; you've got the t-shirt, and as you forgive, you're telling God your ready for Him to bless you as never before.

Search your heart and ask God: "Who is holding up my blessing?" You may be saying, "But this woman just won't submit!" Has it occurred to you that a woman's ability to submit to her husband sometimes depends on her husband's submission to God? And ladies, maybe he's acting the fool, but as you fix your fool his dinner, give it to God and say, "I'm going to do it even though I don't feel like it, because God has called me to it!" The devil doesn't like that.

Satan laughs his head off when we let unforgiveness and selfishness ruin our relationships. The grass isn't greener on the other side; and what looks like grass is actually Astroturf. You might think holding onto your hurts and going on to someone else is the right way to go, but if the grass really is greener somewhere else, the water bill is higher! Instead, try forgiving each other, and watch out because God's blessings are going to knock you over! Remember, a forgiving spirit produces prayers that prevail. Only unforgiveness can stop your prayers of faith.

> *The grass isn't greener on the other side; and what looks like grass is actually Astroturf.*

Have you been praying for a breakthrough but haven't been experiencing it? Do you reach out to God and find the heavens as brass? Are you going through a test that you've taken over and over and should have passed by now? Forgive!

God is saying, "I'm not busy getting your miracle ready; I'm getting *you* ready for *it!*"

You have to set the pace by forgiving; use that as an acronym—PACE.

P is for *Practice reconciliation*—*instant reconciliation*, as soon as you mess up and have something in your heart that you need to let go, ask for forgiveness from God right there on the spot. Don't put it off till tonight or tomorrow. Couples, don't you dare go to sleep without forgiving each other! P: practice instant reconciliation.

A is for *Adopt forgiving others into your daily prayer life.* When you pray, ask God to forgive your debts as you forgive those who are debtors to you. Ask God for forgiveness and to help you forgive others.

C is for *Correct your faults before attempting to correct the faults of others.* People may be responding to you because of the way you behave. If lots of people are hurting you, it may be because of the way you treat them; get the plank out of your eye!

E is for *Examine yourself for things that bother you about other people.* Be introspective; ask God to show you when you're doing things wrong, and especially to forgive you when you mess up.

Remember Mark 11:24-26:

Therefore I say to you, whatever things you ask when you pray, believe that you receive them, and you have them. And whenever you stand praying, if you have anything against anyone, forgive him, that your Father in heaven may also forgive you your trespasses. But if you do not forgive, neither will your Father in heaven forgive you.

It's the Word of God, and it has the answers for your problems. If blessings are being held up in your life, make absolutely, positively sure that you have forgiven! Set the pace! Practice instant reconciliation; adopt forgiving others into your daily prayer life; correct your faults before attempting to correct those in others around you; examine yourself for things that bother you when you see them in other people.

God will forgive you, but you must do the same. It is the key to being free of a prison of unforgiveness. You're the one who built your walls; you can take them down. Forgive!

Let's pray:

"*Father in the name of Jesus, I come now asking that you would first forgive me of all and any of my sins, but most of all help me to forgive those who have harmed me. I can fool others but I cannot fool you so I'm believing that not only have you heard this prayer but you've also answered it and I thank you now. Free me of any hurts, harms or harassments that will hinder me from receiving your best in Jesus' name! Amen.*"

CHAPTER SEVEN

THE MARK OF A CHRISTIAN

If you don't know what persecution is, I pray that by the end of this section, you will not only understand it, but you will have learned how to overcome it. I have three personal principles that are full of power and will be instrumental in allowing us, the people of God, to have the victory.

Matthew 5:1 says, "And seeing the multitudes, He went up on a mountain, and when He was seated, His disciples came to Him." Here is a quick side note for you; rabbis taught in a sitting manner, illustrating Jesus' status as *the* teacher. In the main text, which is commonly known as the Beatitudes or the Sermon on the Mount. Matthew 5:2-10:

> Blessed are the poor in spirit, for theirs is the kingdom of heaven. Blessed are those who mourn, for they shall

be comforted. Blessed are the meek, for they shall inherit the earth. Blessed are those that hunger and thirst for righteousness, for they shall be filled. Blessed are the merciful, for they shall obtain mercy. Blessed are the pure in heart, for they shall see God. Blessed are the peacemakers, for they shall be called the sons of God. Blessed are those who are persecuted for righteousness' sake, for theirs is the kingdom of heaven. Blessed are you when they revile and persecute you, and say all kinds of evil against you falsely for My sake. Rejoice and be exceedingly glad, for great is your reward in heaven, for so they persecuted the prophets who were before you.

The first principle that I want to share with you is that those who live in a Godly manner are promised persecution. Another way of saying this is, when you begin to live for God, and God begins to live through you, people will begin to persecute you. This implies something that some of you may find disturbing: if you're a child of God and you have never been persecuted, you may not be God's child at all.

What does the word *persecute* mean? Persecution is harassment designed to injure you, to grieve you, or to afflict you. Persecution is instead of someone naively talking about you, they slander your name and lie about you—to harass and hurt you. Why would they do that? Why would the enemy have them hit one button, and if it doesn't make you go off, have them hit another and another? The purpose is to grieve you, to mess up your spirit, to agitate you, and, ultimately, to get you out of the spirit and into the flesh.

More than just harassing in a manner designed to injure, grieve, or afflict, persecution is specifically doing things to those who differ in origin, who differ in religion, or who differ in social outlook from the persecutor. If you stand out as different in your environment, persecution will follow.

Jesus teaches two things in Matthew: character and conduct. That's why the Bible says He took them from among the multitudes and sat them down and began to show them the difference between the way they should behave and the multitudes; the multitude are symbolic to the world. Jesus took them from among the multitudes to teach them the Beatitudes. He told them that since they had come out of the multitudes, they ought to act differently, live differently, and respond differently than the world. He told them to expect persecution because they were different, but they were no better than the people of the multitudes.

Because you are no longer in the world doesn't mean you are better than those who are unsaved. If it were not for God's grace and mercy, none of us would have any hope for salvation! That's why I can have mercy towards others—because I understand that God has shown mercy to me, and that although I'm no longer like my coworkers, family members, or neighbors, I'm no better than they are in His sight. I still act like them way too much! I get angry just as they do; I hold grudges just as they do; I resent others, am greedy, and lust after things, just as they do.

However, just as He did with the disciples, Jesus is calling us from among the multitudes, and so we should be different. And when you decide to be different, persecution follows.

Have you experienced persecution because you're different? Let me tell you: there are people out there that don't like you, and you don't understand why they dislike you. They don't like you because you're different, and they see something in you they lack. Ultimately, they don't like you because they actually want what you have—they want to be different like you are! When people lie about you, talk about you behind your back, and slander your name—while all the time smiling to your face—they are stabbing you in the back because they want to take your place; they know how you used to be, and now they see a difference. They know you're different, and they want it.

I have found out that it is a good thing when people begin to persecute you. Wherever you go the respect of Christ should follow you. When you come into a room, dirty jokes being told ought to cease; when you enter a conversation, conviction should come with you—not because of you, but because of Christ inside you! When God begins to live through your life, you can expect to eat lunch by yourself sometimes. You may get to the point where those around you are pulling you down, rather than building you up, you might have to eat alone. We must get fed up with all of the foolishness and garbage that's out there. When He's living through you, you'll get to a point where you're sick and tired of foolishness.

I used to cry out and get very upset because it seemed as though everyone was talking about me. "Lord," I'd say, "why is everyone talking about me? I'm trying to do the right thing!" However, the more they talked about me, the more I came to understand that they were doing it because there was something different in me. And when you're different, you have to expect persecution.

You're not going to fit in with the crowd when He's inside you. So stop trying! Thank God that the crowd doesn't include you; you'd stagnate and be polluted if they did! You're not "holier than thou;" you're more serious about God.

We are persecuted because we are different—not better. Living for God—being different—involves doing what seems strange to the world, and that is a teaching of maturity. It isn't a teaching for the person who just wants to show up at church; it's a teaching for someone who says, "All of me belongs to You!" It's a teaching for the people that say, "I'm tired of playing

We are persecuted because we are different—not better.

church." It's for those who are ready to be the man or woman that God called them to be, who are willing to give when others take, to love when others hate, and to help when others abuse and persecute.

Understand that living a different life is sometimes quite difficult. Jesus says we are to turn the other cheek; we are to bless those that spitefully use us. We overcome the way those who don't follow God treat us by reacting to them as God would have us react—going with them two miles instead of one, giving them your shirt when they steal your jacket, blessing them when they persecute you.

Sometimes that's very difficult to do. I've often been in situations where I begged God to let me lay aside my changes just for a moment so that I can teach someone what happens when they betray me. Just for a moment! However, we are no longer part of the multitudes; we're different, but we're no better.

You are no better than they are. But you *are* different.

So now that we know persecution is going to come, you must make sure that you know how to handle it. And let me add this: the truth is persecution in our time will not be restricted to sinners. We will be victimized by persecutors that will lie about us, disrespect us, and slander our names, and it will happen not just with sinners but right inside the Church! There are "player-haters" right in the Church; people in your church are persecuting you because of what God's doing inside of you. Jesus warns his disciples, and I think we can take that warning too—persecution is not only going to come from the world.

So here is a step for avoiding persecution: do not become a persecutor! Adopt an attitude that says, "Don't come to me with foolishness about my brother or sister; I don't have time to judge anyone else because God is still working on me!" Tell them, "I don't have time to find fault in anybody else; I'm trying to get myself together right now." Why is it that people feel they can come right to you about foolishness regarding your brothers and sisters in Christ? Don't hang around your church, trying to figure out who is real; just make sure *you're* real!

Remember, you're no better than anyone else; you're different, and if God takes His grace and mercy away for one moment, you're exactly like everyone else.

So what do you do when people bring garbage to you? Take it to the garbage can! If you're the victim of persecution, if people have been lying about you, slandering you, and hurting you, God is telling you not to get mad but to get excited, because that means you're maturing in Him. It means you're growing up, and those around you can tell the difference; you're changing. It means that you can measure how you're doing in your life by counting your critics and by numbering the people that you used to hang out with but with whom you no longer fit. They don't call you on the telephone; they aren't inviting you to the movies anymore. You're different now.

Here is the reason you'll be—and should be!—persecuted: "Blessed are those who are persecuted for righteousness' sake, for theirs is the kingdom of heaven," Matthew 5:10. You're going to be persecuted because you're called to be different. You are in the world, but you're not *of* the world!

When I was in high school, a new girl came to my school. Her name was Daisy Chan, and she was from China. She was very smart, but her family didn't have much money, and it was easy to tell this from the way she dressed. Her hair wasn't like ours—it was very straight—and her eyes were slanted, and her clothes were out of style. She was very petite, and she couldn't hit the ball over the net in physical education class.

What am I saying? When she walked into our classroom, persecution was guaranteed, because she was different from everyone else in my class. Every time you go into a sinful, worldly environment, people should instantly realize that you are different. And when they discover you're not just pretending and that you really are different, expect persecution.

It's time to take a stand. Some of us can't be who He has called us to be because we don't want anyone to talk about us. But as I've said before, they are talking about you anyway—you're different! You are in the world, but you are not of the world! Be persecuted for righteousness' sake, for being different. Look to the hills . . .

When you decide you want to be different, to pursue righteousness, people will begin persecuting you as they see you changing. You're life is changing; you can't wait for Sunday morning to seek God anymore! You can't wait for the mid-week service, or your Bible study to study His word. You're tithing regularly and loving it, and every time you can, you're giving.

I'm a living example. As soon as I made up my mind and asked the Lord to make me more than just an average preacher, an average pastor, to use me to teach His people about living in the kingdom, my persecution went to a whole new level!

It is sad, but we actually have Christians in church who are standing in the way of others being saved, because they are releasing condemnation when they think they are releasing conviction. It's not your job as a Christian to condemn the world! It's your job to let God use your life to bring about *conviction*. That's one of the major gripes of the world against the Church—we condemn when we think we're convicting. But condemnation pushes people away from God, and conviction draws a person to God. Rather than telling them they're going to hell, try telling them how they can turn their lives around and experience what you're experiencing—God's blessings because you've chosen to seek Him first.

The Church is responsible for shooting our wounded. How can we have so many small gossip groups and yet be short on intercessors. We can't get people together for a prayer meeting or on a prayer line, but at home we'll

You release conviction when you realize what God's done for you.

get on the phone to pull down our brothers and sisters! We're condemning when we think—or tell ourselves—we're convicting.

Conviction is released when you realize what God's done for you—when you make the decision to be different, to pursue righteousness. The Holy Spirit will convict through you when you show mercy to those who, just as you, don't deserve it. You may be trying to measure yourself against those who are unsaved, and you are different; but when compared to Jesus, you have infinitely far to go, just as they do.

Let me show you another principle. The primary text is Luke 18:9-14, which says:

Also He spoke this parable to some who trusted in themselves that they were righteous and despised others: "Two men went up the temple to pray, one a Pharisee and the other a tax collector. The Pharisee stood and prayed thus with himself, 'God, I thank You that I am not like other men—extortioners, unjust, adulterers, or even this tax collector. I fast twice a week; I give tithes of all that I possess.' And the tax collector,

LOOK TO THE HILLS . . .

standing afar off, would not so much as raise his eyes to heaven, but beat his breast, saying, 'God, be merciful to me, a sinner!' I tell you, this man went down to his house justified rather than the other; for everyone who exalts himself will be humbled, and he who humbles himself will be exalted."

I find this fascinating! We have two people praying, and the first one begins by saying how thankful he is that he isn't this and that he's not that; and then he looks over to another person in church, and he's thankful he's not even like *that*! He's praying to God, but his eyes are on *man*. He's just tooting his own horn. Understand that rules and regulations don't make relationship!

While the first guy is praying about all that he does and doesn't do, and who he's like and who he's not, the other one is saying, "Lord, I know I've messed up! I know I've done wrong, and I need your mercy. Be merciful to me, please!" The Bible tells us that the tax collector went home justified rather than the Pharisee who'd been in church all his life and knew the rules and regulations.

Are you understanding the principle here? Jesus is telling us that our rightness with Him has everything to do with the condition of our hearts and understanding the mercy of God but little or nothing to do with the rules we keep.

Here is another mystery for you: I've told you the reason for persecution—that you're persecuted because you're in the world but not of it, and because you're persecuted for righteousness' sake—but here's the deal; dealing with persecution involves doing the same things that will get you persecuted!

Pursue righteousness! Being righteous doesn't mean you're perfect, it means you are in right standing with God. However, when you're pursuing righteousness, persecution will come.

How do you deal with the persecution? Now that you know it's coming, when it does arrive, first of all make sure that you haven't actually done anything to cause the persecution. Are they persecuting you because of your hunger for God, or are they persecuting you because you're David and they're Saul? Next, make sure you haven't said anything wrong—that you haven't participated in bring-

Remember that real persecution isn't about you; it's about Him in you.

ing down a brother or sister, for instance. Finally, make sure that you don't retaliate in the flesh. Lay hands on yourself and ask for help from God!

This one can be the hardest; you cannot retaliate in the flesh. It's difficult to love your enemies! It's hard to do good to people who are hurting you. So be sure you're right with God, that you haven't thought, said, or done anything wrong to jus-tify being persecuted—except pursued righteousness. Then make sure you don't retaliate in the flesh. That's it; that's how you deal with it. Remember that real persecution isn't about you; it's about Him in you.

One of my favorite examples is Joseph. The Bible tells us that while Joseph was in Potipher's house, Potipher's wife desired him, and he resisted her. However, she made up a story and told it to her husband, and Joseph was thrown into prison. Did he do anything wrong? No, but he still went to prison.

Sometimes God lets you go through persecution so that He can get glory from your situation. Remember, it's not about you. You have to get your eyes off of you! It isn't you they don't like; it's God that's on the inside of you. Deep down, they know it's too late to stop you. They have a sneaky suspicion that God's ready to do something in your life!

> *God will take care of your enemies; your job is to pray for them!*

He's going to bless you when you're persecuted for His sake! God will take care of your enemies; your job is to pray for them! If you pray for them, God will not only deal with them His way, He'll set a table before you in their presence. He'll bless you right in front of them, despite everything they can do to you!

The key is giving it to God. After you have done all, stand! Tell yourself, "Don't go there!" Don't retaliate in the flesh. Your enemies seem to hurt you, but in the long run they help you. Your enemies make you live right! They help keep you holy.

I used to think that everyone was like my sweet mother: Deaconess Earlie Mae Brister, who is the nicest person I know. Anyone who can't get along with her is full of the devil! I used to think everyone was like her, but then I read 1 Peter 3:13-17, which says:

> And who is he who will harm you if you become followers of what is good? But even if you suffer for righteousness sake you are blessed. And do not be afraid of

their threats, nor be troubled. But sanctify the Lord God in your hearts, and always be ready to give a defense to everyone who asks you a reason for the hope that is in you, with meekness and fear; having a good conscience, that when they defame you as evil doers, those who revile your good conduct in Christ may be ashamed. For it is better, if it is the will of God, to suffer for doing good than for doing evil.

Your enemies see that you are meek, and they assume that you're weak. But don't take meekness for granted! Meekness is strength under control!
1 Peter 4:14 says:

If you are reproached for the name of Christ, blessed are you, for the Spirit of glory and of God rests upon you. On their part He is blasphemed, but on your part He is glorified. But let none of you suffer as a murderer, a thief, an evildoer, or as a busybody in other peoples' matters. Yet if anyone suffers as a Christian, let him not be ashamed, but let him glorify God this matter. For the time has come for judgment to begin at the house of God; and if it begins with us first, what will be the end of those who do not obey the gospel of God? Now if the righteous one is scarcely saved, where will the ungodly and the sinners appear? Therefore let those who suffer according to the will of God commit their souls to Him, as to a faithful Creator.

Because you are currently doing good doesn't mean you will be exempt from suffering persecution, and, ultimately, when you begin to live righteously, you begin to suffer even more. But then he also tells you

> *Don't take meekness for granted! Meekness is strength under control!*

what to do about it. For as you are persecuted, He is lifted up; on their part He is blasphemed, but on yours He is glorified. Be glad when you are persecuted, because it shows you're committed to being different, and inheriting the kingdom of heaven.

Now let's pray concerning persecution.

"Father in the name of Jesus Christ, I thank you that your word is true. I understand that Godly living is promised persecution. I pray Father that you will give me the necessary strength to endure the persecution I've been experiencing. I even pray for my persecutors. I know you are true to your word and I thank you for the victory in Jesus' name. Amen."

CHAPTER EIGHT

"FORGETTING THOSE THINGS. . . ."

At this point, I'd like to discuss setbacks. In Philippians 3:12-16 you'll find these words:

> Not that I have already attained, or am already perfected; but I press on, that I may lay hold that for which Christ Jesus has also laid hold of me. Brethren, I do not count myself to have apprehended; but one thing I do, forgetting those things which are behind and reaching forward to those things which are ahead, I press toward the goal for the prize of the upward call of God in Christ Jesus. Therefore let us, as many as are mature, have this mind; and if in anything you think otherwise, God will reveal even this to you. Nevertheless, to the degree that we have already attained, let us walk by the same rule, let us be of the same mind.

Paul is saying that he realizes despite all of his accomplishments, he still has not *arrived*. However, he also lets us know that instead of dwelling on the things of the past, he reaches forward to what lies ahead—the future, rather than the past. The image he uses to describe this reaching is similar to that of a runner in a race, straining every muscle and even leaning forward in order to be the first one over the finish line.

We're talking about setbacks, and the first thing we learn is that we must forget the things that are behind us and press toward the goal—the prize, the high calling—that is in Christ Jesus. We all experience setbacks, and we will throughout our lives. They are inevitable. It doesn't matter how much you love the Lord, or how much you fast and pray!

I understand that not everyone will intensely identify with what I'm saying, but there are others, those of you who have suffered so much pain and trauma that new injuries hardly even hurt anymore, to whom this is a word in due season. Setbacks are inevitable, but that doesn't mean that you're life should be dominated by them. Some of us have experienced significant setbacks because of abuse when we were children, or rejection by loved ones; perhaps you were abandoned, or you've been bitterly stabbed in the back by someone you trusted intimately. Perhaps some of you are even feeling the restraining guilt of having been a perpetrator, rather than a victim.

This book is designed with an over-all purpose in mind, and it is the same one to which I feel my preaching ministry is called. In the age in which we live, the way you think about yourself is vital. I feel God has called me to help believers change the way in which they think about themselves, because for good or ill, the way you see yourself is the way the devil sees you. If you see yourself as defeated, so will he; but if you see yourself as more than a conqueror through Christ Jesus, that is how the enemy will see you! We're going to be developing new attitudes in this book, helping you to think of yourself as a warrior of Christ—a runner who is bound and determined to see the race through to the end.

Many of us have experienced setbacks that are holding us back because we are looking back! And in a race, when you look back, you loose ground. That's why Paul says that whatever you've experienced in life— both good and bad—it's time to stop crying about it. It's time to

In a race, when you look back you lose ground.

get over it and reach towards the mark of the high calling.

During the time of a major setback in my life, I received a phone call from one of the couples in my ministry. I answered the phone and the husband starts talking: "Bishop, you'll never know how much you have changed our lives, me and my wife— our whole situation is different!" I don't even remember what I said that blessed them. The wife gets on and says "Bishop, I appreciate you so much. I'm an intercessor; I'm always praying for you." She didn't know I was in the middle of a major setback.

After I had heard and received the encouragement she and her husband had for me, I was ready to attack the devil and let him know that everything I had been going through *was* worth it! My labor in the Lord was not in vain, and neither is yours, regardless of the setback you might be experiencing now.

I am sharing this real life situation because people who are going through setbacks need to know that there is hope! It's time for a comeback! Stop complaining about how rough it is and make up your mind that you will believe God and be used for His glory.

The reason you can't sit back in your setback is that someone needs you! It doesn't matter how far you think you've sunk into the pit of despair; it doesn't matter how badly you failed or how tragic your circumstances are or how badly you're hurting—somebody needs you, needs your testimony, to help them get our of their desperate setback. We all need each other.

The reason you can't sit back in your setback is that someone needs you!

I know you can help someone. I know that if you share what you've overcome to someone going through a rough time, you can help them. You might be the one to break them out of their setback and in turn help them minister to someone else.

I'm going to give you the key: the best way to get out of your own setback is to reach out and help someone else.

When you're in a setback, you must take your eyes off of yourself and put them on God—understand that everything you go through is for a reason, and that the same God you followed in will bring you out. You must realize that even when you're down, there's someone lower—somebody who needs you to reach out and give them hope, because they need you! The majority of the things you go through isn't for you anyway; it's so you can share your victories with someone else!

The first step in overcoming setbacks is getting your eyes off of you and getting them on God; you've got to ask Him who is it around you that need you to share your testimony of the times

> *The best way to get out of your own setback is to reach out and help someone else!*

God has brought you out? If He brought you out, He'll bring them out, and He'll bring you out again! His glory is revealed when you emerge victorious.

1 Samuel 30:1-2 says:

> Now it came to pass that when David and his men came to Ziklag, on the third day, that Amalekites had invaded the South and Ziklag, attacked Ziklag and burned it with fire, and had taken captive the women and those who were there from small to great; they did not kill anyone, but carried them away and went their way.

Talk about a setback! The interesting part is that they didn't kill anyone, but instead they carried them all away— they took them captive. And that's what the enemy does; he will often take things that he can later dangle in front of you. Verse 3 says, "So David and his men came to the city, which was, burned with fire; and their wives, their sons, and their daughters had been taken captive." In the next verse it says that "David and the people that were with him lifted up their voices and wept, until they had no more power to weep." Some of you know what it feels like to cry until you can't cry anymore. David lost his two wives in the raid, and the people considered stoning him because they were so distressed. However, David strengthened himself in the Lord his God.

There will be times when you experience setbacks that those around you just want to kill you, and you'll have to get your encouragement, your strength, right from God.

We'll come back to David's situation in a moment, but I want to encourage you to know that your comeback is going to be greater than you can imagine. That might only confirm what God has already told some of you, but if you accept this word, something in your life will break open! You're going to come out of your season of despair, and you're going to enter your season of breakthrough.

> *You're comeback is going to be better than you can even imagine.*

You're comeback is going to be better than you can even imagine, and it's very important that you don't listen to the enemy and take a step backward. You must take a stand and believe God for your comeback.

The enemy likes to play tricks on your mind. He likes to make you think you're the only one that has ever been through whatever it is you're going through—so you might be surprised to learn that some of the biggest names in the Bible also messed up big time and had to have major comebacks.

One fellow I'm thinking of is Abram; he had a beautiful wife, while they were in Egypt, he told his wife Sarah to lie to the Pharaoh and tell him that she was his sister. A mighty man of God told his wife to lie because he was afraid!

Genesis tells the story of Abram and Sarah's situation and how Abram gave in to his fear; however, in spite of this God later changed his name to Abraham and made a promise to him that he'd be the father of many nations. He was the father of the Jewish people. He messed up in chapter 12, but by chapter 17, God is establishing a covenant with him, which tells me that even though you mess up, God can and will use you in spite of your mess up.

Moses is another good example. In Exodus we learn that he *murders* a man, and yet God still uses him to lead the Children of Israel out of Egypt in Exodus 12. Rahab, a prostitute, saves Joshua and Caleb in Joshua chapter 2—and though she probably couldn't remember the names of all the men she'd slept with, she is actually listed in the lineage of David and the Lord Jesus Christ in Matthew 1:6! Can you imagine that the God of all the universe was born through a lineage that included a redeemed harlot! And then there's Peter; in John 18, Peter starts off by cutting a man's ear off as they're coming to take Jesus, and then later, he denies that he knows Jesus three times! This is after he said that he'd die for Jesus. However, on the day of Pentecost, do you know what God does? He takes away Peter's shame, and uses him to preach on the day of Pentecost, bringing three thousand people to salvation.

When you experience a setback, you can either give up, or you can believe God for a comeback. If you haven't figured it out yet, understand that God is a God of comebacks! He's in the redemption business! Get out from under your cloud of condemnation and self-pity. You have to learn to see yourself, your faults and failures, from the Father's viewpoint. It is vital that you begin to see yourself as God sees you, because the way you see yourself is the way the enemy sees you.

Sometimes we forget that our God knows the end from the beginning. He had your redemption set up before you were born, and before you ever messed up, he already had made provision for your cleanup. You see, your setback is actually a setup for redemption!

God is a God of comebacks!

The Word of God is full of examples of people who have messed up, but the key is in their attitudes after they experienced their setbacks. David and Saul are two men that experienced two completely different outcomes—not because one messed up and the other did not, but instead because of the way David dealt with his failures versus the way Saul dealt with his. If you pay attention, you'll see that David did more wicked things than Saul did! What was the difference? Saul messed up, and he said, "Oh well; I blew it," but when David failed, his heart was broken and he repented. The Bible says that David was a man after God's own heart.

The way you deal with your setbacks illustrates what kind of relationship you have with God—when you mess up, do you feel bad that you blew it, or does it bother you? Do you feel convicted, dirty, or unworthy?

Nathan the prophet came to David after he had sinned with Bathsheba, and David's reaction was to say, "Have mercy upon me, O God, according to Your loving kindness; according to the multitude of your tender mercies, blot out my transgressions." He asks God to wash him of his iniquity and to cleanse him. Listen to his heart, starting again in verse 2 of Psalm 51:

> Wash me thoroughly from my iniquity, and cleanse me from my sin. For I acknowledge my transgressions, and my sin is always before me. Against You, You only, have I sinned, and done this evil in Your sight—that You may be found just when You speak, and blameless when You judge. I was brought forth in iniquity, and in sin my mother conceived me. Behold, You desire truth in the inward part, and in the hidden part You will make me to know wisdom. Purge me with hyssop, and I shall be clean; wash me and I shall be whiter than snow. Make me to hear joy and gladness, that the bones You have broken may rejoice. Hide Your face from my sins, and blot out all my iniquities. Create in me a clean heart, O God, and renew a steadfast spirit within me. Do not cast me away from Your presence, and do not take Your Holy Spirit from me.

David then goes on to say that he'd happily tell of God's ways—His redemption—to anyone and everyone, and that he'd tell others of what God did for him, He would do for them also. He says that everywhere he goes, he'll tell people that God is a God of mercy and love. He's the God of another chance.

Some of what you're going through may not be for your personal benefit. God wants you to share His victory through you with others! His mercy is powerful enough to repair all your messes; and change you in the process. He doesn't want to cover up your mistakes; He wants to change you—to make a difference in your life.

He loves you so much! He needs you. How can I say that? You're the only one He has to do what He has destined you to do. He created you, and nobody else can do exactly what He has designed you to do. When He created you, He broke the mold; He tells you in His Word that you're fearfully and wonderfully made! Your pastor

> *There are people out there, every day, that only you can reach.*

can't touch everyone. There are people out there, every day, that only you can reach. God needs you! That's why the car wreck didn't kill you, or the divorce didn't cause you to have a nervous breakdown.

You must think differently about yourself, because the way you see yourself is the way the enemy sees you. You need to learn to see yourself as God sees you—a redemptive work in progress, a unique vessel for His ministry on this earth! God is a God of comebacks, and He's already got one ready for your setback. Whatever you're going through, is another chance for Him to show that He is Lord over every circumstance in your life.

You are an overcomer!

Pray with me this unusual prayer:

"Father in the name of Jesus, thank you for every setback I've experienced. Thank you for those who were responsible (in the natural) for my setback, because I now have come to know you in a way that I would not have, had I not experienced the setback. So thank you for your provision and your promises, in Jesus' name! Amen."

CHAPTER NINE

JUST WHAT THE DR. ORDERED

In this chapter, many of you, will discover why some of the problems and situations in your life are lasting overtime. I believe that we sometimes go through tests that should have ended long ago. Because of our attitudes and actions, it appears that we have been playing with God. We are in a very serious season now, and I want you to understand this because the Bible says judgment starts at the house of God first. We can walk in deception for so long that we subconsciously think that we can deceive God.

> There are many people who have fallen in love with church, but have not fallen in love with Jesus.

I want to discuss overcoming prayerlessness. There are many people who have fallen in love with church, but have not fallen in love with Jesus. There are a lot of people drawn to religion that have not solidified their relationship with Jesus.

It is imperative that we are where we are supposed to be. We should all ask the Holy Spirit not to give us rest until our prayer life moves from mere desire to daily discipline. If we were all where we were supposed to be in our relationship with God, I promise you, we would not be going through some of the tests, trials, and tribulations we go through.

Many of us know beyond a shadow of a doubt that prayer changes things. I'm confident that there are not very many of you reading this who remain unconvinced as to the effectiveness of prayer. But we fall into the slick schemes of the enemy—by letting him dictate our agenda so that we don't take time to pray.

We have not given ourselves to a life of prayer. It doesn't matter what your title is; it doesn't matter what your position is; it doesn't matter how long you have been saved; it doesn't matter how many scriptures you can quote—if you are a believer and you don't have a daily prayer life with God, you are a heathen. I'm going to prove it to you in Scripture.

> *You are only as strong as your prayer life.*

You are only as strong as your prayer life. You can gauge your spiritual maturity by your understanding of the importance of finding time for God in your hustle-and-bustle life. I'm going to present some principles to you, so pay attention. Matthew 6:5 says:

And when you pray, you shall not be like the hypocrites. For they love to pray standing in the synagogues and on the corners of the streets, that they may be seen by men. Assuredly, I say to you, they have their reward. But you, when you pray, go into your room, and when you have shut your door, pray to your Father who is in the secret place; and your Father who sees in secret will reward you openly. And when you pray, do not use vain repetitions as the heathens do. For they think that they will be heard for their many words. Therefore do not be like them. For your Father knows the things you have need of before you ask Him.

Now that He's told us how *not* to pray, Jesus gives us the way we are supposed to pray. We call it the Lords prayer, beginning in verse 9:

In this manner, therefore, pray: Our Father in heaven, hallowed be Your name. Your kingdom come. Your will be done on earth as it is in heaven. Give us this day our daily bread, and forgive us our debts as we forgive our debtors. And do not lead us into temptation, but deliver us from the evil one. For Yours is the kingdom and the power and the glory forever. Amen.

I want you to understand this; we have been taught over many years that this is the Lord's Prayer. In a sense it is, but this was not the prayer the Lord prayed. Jesus did not have to pray this prayer, but this was a *model* for teaching *us* to pray. Ultimately, this is designed to teach us not to just say words but also to embrace the principles behind it. Jesus is teaching principles.

Some of us are at a standstill, and some of us have gone backwards because we have not understood the importance of having a enemy devotional prayer life with the Lord Jesus Christ. The enemy doesn't care how much you come to church; he doesn't care how much scripture you can memorize; he doesn't care how fast you go up the supernatural ladder of success.

But if he can keep you from praying, he knows that he'll hinder your spiritual life and relationship with God. As you establish daily devotions with God, you'll find that you will be unable to do certain things that your flesh might want you to do—you just can't do them anymore!

I promise you that the person who is bound by his will and not God's will is a person who has not been praying.

> *I promise you that the person who is bound by his will and not God's will is a person who has not been praying.*

When you really enter into prayer, your flesh comes into subjection to the will of God; that's why your flesh doesn't want to pray! Can you identify with me when I say that I can go all day perfectly wide awake, but when I kneel down to pray, suddenly I can't stay awake. Ironic, isn't it?

However, it's not simple irony at work here; no, there is a war going on. Prayer is warfare. Every form of prayer is warfare. When you discipline yourself to pray, what you're saying to God is that you're not going to try to deal with issues in your life on your own, but you're bringing Him in on the matter. You may have trouble dealing with your co-workers and you say, "I don't want to deal with those folks on my own, God! I need Your help!" When you get to a point where you begin to pray, you take God's finger and point it at the issue. And there isn't anything that God cannot deal with that goes on in your life.

Many of us, complain, murmur, loose sleep, our blood pressure goes up—all over stuff that we can't do anything about. A songwriter says, "Oh what needless pain we bear, all because we do not carry everything to God in prayer."

You may be surprised to learn that there is a rising number of Christians who do not pray. Ask yourself, "Do I have a regular prayer life?" "Do I really? I know you prayed before; remember that time when you got into trouble? Do you ask God's finger to point at every situation in your life?

I don't want to be a preacher who prays; I want to be a person of prayer prayer who preaches! You shouldn't want to be a choir member who prays; you should be a person of prays who sings in the choir!

We need to get to the point where we say, "God, move me to a point of daily discipline in prayer!" The disciples said, "Lord, teach us to pray." Lay hands on yourself and say, "Lord, teach me to pray. Teach me to pray. Not *how* to pray, but bring me to a point that I *will* pray!"

The old covenant focused on the external practices of devotion, but Jesus presents devotion as a matter of the heart. In the Old Testament, devotion was all external.

That's what Jesus did; He contrasted sincere, heartfelt devotion with the external, hypocritical, pretentious practices of the Pharisees. That's what He shows us in the Lord's Prayer; He warns His disciples against allowing even genuine good works to distract from wholehearted devotion to Him.

Your flesh doesn't want to hear this!

You need to overcome prayerlessness, and when you do, the enemy won't be able to run rampant through your home and have his way with your wife, or your husband, or your children, or your job. The enemy won't be able to break you down with the issues that would normally get on your nerves, making your flesh so prominent that no one can see the Spirit of God on the inside of you. But when you get to that point where you say, "Lord, I'm tired of handling stuff on my own; I want you involved in every situation in my life," you'll be set free.

> *You need to overcome prayerlessness, and when you do, the enemy won't be able to run rampant through your home*

The enemy likes to mess up relationships by keeping you from prayer. There are times when you and your husband or wife will go back and forth for days or weeks, and both of you know that all you have to do is come together and pray—because when you do, something happens! You won't be able to mistreat each other if you get to the point where you just *pray*! The enemy wants you to get caught up in church work without devotion to Jesus Christ. No devotion—that's a word for the entire body of Christ. We are lacking devotion.

In Matthew 6:5, Jesus tells us that when we pray, we're not to be like the hypocrites; that is, pretenders—people who are faking it. Hypocrites love to pray in prominent places so that men can see them, but Jesus says that they have their reward. Because really, what is their motive? It is to be seen by man. So when men see them, they get their reward—that's it. They get the praise of men, but what we're after is devotion to God!

We have to get to a point, saints, that prayer moves in our lives from desire to daily discipline. First of all, you have to develop the desire. Many of us don't pray because we don't have the desire. We don't understand what prayer is. Prayer is not just going to God as though He

> *Prayer is intimacy. Prayer is fellowshipping with the God of the universe.*

is a sanctified Santa Claus. Prayer is intimacy. Prayer is fellowshipping with the God of the universe, the Lord of lords, and the King of kings.

We need to get to the point where we love to pray. Sometimes I can't wait till I can get in my car and turn the radio off; it's just God and me. When you pray, you feel better. When I pray, I walk right. When I pray, I live right. When I pray, that which had me burdened down is lifted. When you get to the point where it is desire, then it has to become daily discipline. But you have to desire it first. It's a wonderful thing to go to God in prayer!

Do you know what it's like to spend time with God and not even realize that thirty minutes have passed? When you begin getting to that point, depression can't get a hold of you; oppression can't get a grip on you; the spirit of lone-liness has to leave that one-bedroom apartment. And here's the trick; the more you do it—engaging in intimate times with God—the more you will *love* talking to God!

Have you ever been in love before? We say we love Jesus. But when you fall in love with someone, you can't wait for the phone to ring; you can't wait to talk to that person. That's how God feels toward us. But does He say, "You say you love Me, but I haven't heard from you in four days," to you? Does He say, "You say you love me, but we haven't talked since last Sunday" when you finally get around to praying? How strong can a relationship be if you don't talk to the other person? Perhaps you are starting to see what I mean by playing with God.

Jesus warns His disciples against allowing even gen-uine good works to distract them from wholehearted devo-tion. In verse 6 of our text, it says that when you pray, go into your room and pray to your Father in heaven in secret; it says that when you pray to your Father in secret, He will reward you openly. In other words, when you spend time with God, He says that He'll make sure everyone knows you've been spending time together. He says that He'll let others see the evidence of your time together by the blessings He sows into your life.

Something is wrong if you are still believing in God and waiting on something that you've been praying for over the last three years. God says, "No, wait a minute. You can't just ask, ask, ask! You have to do some giving, giving, giving! When you spend some time with Me—give Me what I want—then I'll give you the desires of your heart."

God will make sure people know that you have been spending quality time working on your relationship. When you go into your secret closet, God will openly give you what you've prayed for in secret—for your edification, and more importantly, for His glory. People will say, "How in the world did you get that? Your credit was all messed up." Then you can tell them that you've just been spending some time with Jesus; you've just been having a little talk with Jesus!

I believe that you might have a prompting in your spirit. You've been hearing God say to you, "You need to get up a little earlier. Spend some time with Me." What do you think it is when you wake up thirty minutes before your alarm clock goes off? Don't you know that's the Spirit of God beckoning to you? He's saying, "Can we spend a little time together? Talk to Me about what's going on—tell Me what I already know." He says, "Come, let us reason together." You do know He'll give you wisdom if you ask; how do you think you get it? You talk to Him!

Have you let your spiritual life come to a standstill? Do you know anything more about God than you did four years ago that someone else didn't share with you? Ask yourself, "What's the latest revelation God has given me?" What has He revealed to you lately? Has

If you haven't heard from God lately, it's because He hasn't heard from you!

He shown you anything about your situation that you didn't get from a preacher, or a tape, or a video?

I promise you that if you haven't heard from God lately, it's because He hasn't heard from you!

125

Devotion involves developing an intimate relationship with the living God. Devotion is a matter of developing an intimate relationship and learning to enjoy the warmth of a life that draws us near to His Father's heart. In other words, devotion is a drawing; it's a connection.

My favorite time of day is early in the morning, this is my time of devotion. Before I even leave the house, I have thanked God for a good day and laid out my troubles and problems—all before the enemy can depress me with the day's burdens. I say, "Lord, today is the day of victory for me. I don't know what the enemy is going to do, but I am letting him know that whatever he brings in my life this day, I'll overcome. Thank you that You've already given me the victory!"

Devotion is a matter of developing an intimate relationship with the living God. You have to work at that; you have to strengthen the relationship. You cannot expect your time in church to be enough! You have to burn the midnight oil. You have to get up in the morning. Even though you know God is real, you'll still be surprised what happens. Your life will change instantly! God is saying that if you give Him what He wants, He'll give you what you want! Go to your secret closet; develop an intimate relationship with the living God, learning what it's like to draw near to the heart of the Father.

Many of us sing, talk, read, and discuss issues on or about prayer, but so many of us don't *pray*! Why? Because it hasn't become a desire of our hearts. We haven't understood the joy of going to a holy God in prayer. How is it that something so wonderful, which could change your life, your circumstances, and your environment doesn't get through our thick heads? Because we are bound by a spirit of prayerlessness.

How can you be a swimmer and hate water? How can you be an athlete and not like to exert yourself? How can you eat pancakes with no syrup? How in the world can you eat mustard greens with no corn bread? The point is, how can you be a Christian and not pray?

Lord, teach us to pray! I can hear the Holy Ghost saying, "I miss My time with you." Christianity is *not* about rules and regulations; it's about relationship! It's about the joy of having a one-on-one relationship with the God of creation. He saved you to have fellowship with you. He *saved* you to have *relationship* with you.

I want relationship! I want to be glorified on His behalf. God is saying, "I have so much I want to give you, but I can't give it to you because I can't get you to slow down to ask Me for it!"

Here is something that may bother you: sometimes the enemy is not the sole responsible party for holding up your breakthrough and blessings. It is a lack of discipline on our part, some of us have come to love the contrivance of church, but we don't love Christ. We have come to love the mechanics of our religion, and we have not established a relationship!

Luke 10:38 says:

Now it happened as they went that He entered a certain village; and a certain woman named Martha welcomed Him into her house. And she had a sister called Mary, who also sat at Jesus' feet and heard His word. But Martha was distracted with much serving, and she approached Him and said, "Lord, do You not care that my sister has left me to serve alone? Therefore, tell her to help me." And Jesus answered and said to her, "Martha, Martha, you are worried and troubled about many things. But one thing is needed, and Mary has chosen that good part, which will not be taken away from her."

This is very interesting; Martha serving and Mary sitting. What we have to do is avoid setting the Lord's work as a priority over the Lord's presence. You cannot let doing the Lord's work mean more to you than embracing the Lord's presence. Many of us serve, but we don't sit. Oh, we are busy; we're at church five days a week. Always serving, serving, serving. You cannot set the Lord's work as a priority over the Lord's presence. And that's what prayer does; prayer gets you into His presence.

> *You cannot let doing the Lord's work mean more to you than embracing the Lord's presence.*

That's why Jesus warned them that even good works can distract you from wholehearted devotion. Why can't you pray in the morning? Because you have to go to work, school, or church every morning.

You cannot be working in God's house and not have time for a personal relationship. If all you are doing is working for the kingdom, and never sitting in the kingdom, you can't represent the kingdom. You don't know the King of the kingdom! The way you get to know the King is by sitting, not by serving!

Some of you reading this are involved in every ministry your church has available, as though by using up your time you're ingratiating yourself to God. But when do you have time to sit?

You must avoid setting the Lord's work as a priority over His presence. Who told you to become an usher? Who told you to sing in the choir? Are you doing it out of obligation, or is it something you feel called to do? Have you ever considered that if you were spending time in His presence, He might have shown you where He *really* wanted you to be? Did you join a ministry because that's where your friends are? Or did you join something because that's where God led you?

There are only three types of works: good works, evil works, and dead works, and that's what concerns me about ministry. I feel the Lord is calling us to pray as we never have before—so that our efforts won't be dead works.

Lay hands on yourself and say, "Lord, teach me to pray. God, I have to make sure I am doing what You want me to do." Before you judge someone because they aren't involved in as much as you are, consider whether or not he or she may be sitting before His feet and hearing from Him more than you are! Is she Mary and you're Martha? I promise you, we have men in our churches who were never designed by God to be deacons. We've got some people who were never supposed to be ushers trying to force you into a seat. We have people in the choir that God never called to be in the choir. There *is* one thing that God has called each and every believer to do; He has called us all to pray!

And while you've got a 200-voice choir, your church can't find five people to man the prayer line. What is our motive? Are we afraid that no one will see us praying, whereas if we're up in the choir every week the whole congregation will know what wonderful Christians we are? Who told you to be in the activities you're in now? Was it really God?

> *There is one thing that God has called each and every believer to do: He has called us all to pray!*

We have this church thing set up wrong. As soon as someone gets in the body of Christ, we want to put them to work. They need to sit and hear what God is saying so they'll know what He wants them to do. Sometimes God says, "You aren't supposed to be do anything right now! Just sit here at My feet so I can develop you! Don't worry; I'll show you where you're supposed to be." So when you move, you're not going to do what looks good to man, you'll do what you heard God's Spirit instruct you to do.

Let me suggest something: instead of being at your church seven days a week, you spent time with your three children, or your husband or wife? What if, instead of being in church every time the doors are open, you were at home preventing the enemy from tearing your house up while you're away? What if you took time to check your kids' homework instead of going to the Christian Women's Tupperware meeting? What if you took time to go to your son's baseball game? What if, instead of investing your time in dead works, you sat? What if you didn't let His work be a priority over His presence?

I found out that when you spend time with God in prayer, He develops the gift of discernment in you. When you spend time with God, you find out what is of God and what is not of God. The greatest gift God has given me is the gift of discernment. That's what I need, because I come in contact with so many Christians who are in the flesh. I can tell when someone spends time with God. You can see the presence of God all over them! You can hear God speaking through them. That's why half the folk you come in contact with grieve you; because you are of a different kingdom! They live in the flesh, but you live in His presence.

You have to sit in His presence so you can hear Him speak to you. Read this carefully: I promise that you will never succeed as a Christian until you learn to pray. Your life will always be up and down and in and out until you learn to pray. You have to move from desire to daily discipline.

> *How much of your life do you spend with the One sustaining your life?*

You will never succeed as a Christian until you learn to pray.

What day of the week is it as you read this? There are 1,440 minutes in a day. How many minutes, Christian, have you spent in prayer? How much of your life do you spend with the One sustaining your life? You will not succeed as a Christian until you learn to pray. Everything about you will fail. The enemy hates me; he hates words like this.

Some of you are experiencing something even as you read this; perhaps you can't wait to finish this book so that you can get on your knees and pray. But though you may still be tempted to fall asleep, this time you'll persevere and tell God about everything—and despite getting less sleep, you'll wake up more rested than you have in a long time. You'll begin waking up with joy unspeakable, peace that flows like a river. The enemy is going be upset, because the stuff he had planned to get on your nerves tomorrow isn't going to faze you because you have been spending time with God.

Luke 18:1 says that we ought to pray always and not lose heart—in other words, don't give up. That's why you can't quit, even when getting into a better prayer life is hard.

You cannot have a wholesome relationship with someone if you don't talk to him or her. Two out of three marriages end in divorce not because the people don't love each other; it's because they can't communicate. Poor communication is the number one destroyer of relationships because it causes division—two visions. The two of you don't see things the same way because you're not talking about them.

That's all prayer is—communicating with God. Nothing else connects us with God as prayer does. So if you don't pray, you're not connected. Church attendance doesn't connect you with God. Serving and working in the church doesn't connect you with God. The only thing that connects you with God is prayer. If you have not been praying, you are not connected. Prayer is the vital link.

My desire is that we become a praying body of believers. When we become a praying people, the gossip will diminish. When we become a praying people, the Pharisees will leave. When we become a praying people, we won't judge others. When we become a praying people, spirits of jealousy and anger will no longer find unwitting, powerless believers. When you get in God's presence, when you stand in His presence, the light comes on you.

When you get in His presence, you have to forgive; you can't hold a grudge when you're really in His presence. When you get into His presence, you can't justify. Don't start off by asking God to give you this and give you that. Pray and ask God what you can give away to others, what they may need. Pray that you can encourage others, because you yourself need to be encouraged.

Mark 1:33-35 describes the way Jesus handled prayer. After having healed all of those brought to Him—probably late into the night—He got up early the next morning and departed for a solitary place. What did He do? He prayed.

Jesus, who just finished working miracles the night before, gets up before the sun comes up, and He goes to a solitary place. Now, this is Jesus who had to get up before everyone else to find a secret place, and He was God in the flesh! He said that we are to learn from His example. He got up before everybody else and went to a solitary place—that can be your living room or a bathroom; it can be your office. He got up early with one thing on His mind: Prayer—communication with His Father. This is devotion.

So God before I say good morning to anyone, I want to say good morning to the Holy Spirit. Thank Him for watching over you. It's when you learn to thank God for the small things, that you begin to understand how good God has been to you.

Understand this: You will never succeed as a Christian until you learn to pray, and in this day and age, we need to pray as we never have before! Pray for the desire; pray for the discipline. Pray just to tell God about your day, and as you remember to thank Him and just talk to Him, remember others in your prayers—then you can pray for yourself. Remember: He's saying to you, "Give me what I want"—your devotion—"and I'll give you the desires of your heart."

Look to the hills . . .

AUTHOR CONTACT INFORMATION

For more information please contact:

Darryl S. Brister Ministries
P.O. Box 1526
Harvey, LA 70059-1526

www.dsbrister.org

Toll free: 1-866-PARTAKE